ABSOLUTE TRUTH AND UNBEARABLE PSYCHIC PAIN

CIPS Series on The Boundaries of Psychoanalysis
Series Editor: Fredric T. Perlman, PhD, FIPA

CIPS

CONFEDERATION OF INDEPENDENT PSYCHOANALYTIC SOCIETIES
www.cipsusa.org

The Confederation of Independent Psychoanalytic Societies (CIPS) is the national professional association for the independent component societies of the International Psychoanalytical Association (IPA) in the USA. CIPS also hosts the Direct Member Society for psychoanalysts belonging to other IPA societies. Our members represent a wide spectrum of psycho-analytic perspectives as well as a diversity of academic backgrounds. The CIPS Book Series, The Boundaries of Psychoanalysis, represents the intellectual activity of our community. The volumes explore the internal and external boundaries of psychoanalysis, examining the interrelationships between various psychoanalytic theoretical and clinical perspectives as well as between psychoanalysis and other disciplines.

ABSOLUTE TRUTH AND UNBEARABLE PSYCHIC PAIN
Psychoanalytic Perspectives on Concrete Experience

Edited by
Allan Frosch

Routledge
Taylor & Francis Group

LONDON AND NEW YORK

First published 2012 by Karnac Books Ltd.

Published 2018 by Routledge
2 Park Square, Milton Park, Abingdon, Oxon OX14 4RN
711 Third Avenue, New York, NY 10017, USA

Routledge is an imprint of the Taylor & Francis Group, an informa business

British Library Cataloguing in Publication Data

A C.I.P. for this book is available from the British Library

ISBN-13: 9781855757981 (pbk)

Typeset by V Publishing Solutions Pvt Ltd., Chennai, India

This book is dedicated to the memories of Norbert Freedman, Ph.D., and Laurence J. Gould, Ph.D.

CONTENTS

ACKNOWLEDGEMENTS

Special thanks go to Norbert Freedman who first came up with the idea of a CIPS book series and to Fredric (Rick) Perlman who, as president of CIPS, brought it to the executive board. The board's approval led to the appointment of Meg Beaudoin as the series editor and the formation of a committee to discuss the structure, theme, and possible publisher for the series. I was delighted to be asked to work on this book, and I am grateful for Meg's calm oversight. The recent appointment of Rick as series editor highlights the talent and dedication at CIPS that two such accomplished people—Meg and Rick—would take on the job of series editor. I especially want to thank all the contributors to this book. Their talent, cooperation, and patience made my job as editor that much easier.

ABOUT THE EDITOR AND CONTRIBUTORS

Maxine Anderson, MD, FIPA, has been a psychoanalyst for over thirty-five years, training in both North America (Seattle in the Seventies) and London, England in the late Eighties. She is a training and supervising analyst in the Seattle Psychoanalytic Society and Institute, the Western Branch of the Canadian Psychoanalytic Society (Vancouver, BC), and a founding member and training analyst and supervising analyst of the Northwestern Psychoanalytic Society (Seattle), and a full member of the British Psychoanalytical Society. Recent interests involve Wilfred Bion's work, especially his notions of learning from emotional experience and the forces for and against knowing and growth. Most recently she has begun to integrate the evolutionary perspective of primitive mental states into her psychoanalytic understandings. Maxine lives and works in Seattle.

Alan Bass, PhD, FIPA is a training analyst and faculty member of IPTAR, the New York Freudian Society, the National Psychological Association for Psychoanalysis, and is on the graduate faculty of the New School for Social Research. He is the author of *Difference and Disavowal: The Trauma of Eros* and *Interpretation and Difference: The Strangeness of Care* (both Stanford University Press) and many articles.

Joseph A. Cancelmo, PsyD, FIPA, was president of IPTAR (2008–2010), chair of the IPTAR board of directors, the IPTAR outside advisory board, training and supervising analyst (fellow) and faculty member of IPTAR. Previously, he served as coordinator of adult clinical services and outreach coordinator at IPTAR's Clinical Center (ICC). He is a certified school and clinical psychologist, psychoanalyst, has written articles on diagnosis and clinical technique (most recently, *The Role of the Transitional Realm as an Organizer of Analytic Process: Transitional Organizing Experience*), and co-authored books on parents' relationships with their child care providers (*Child Care for Love or Money: A Guide to Navigating the Parent-Caregiver Relationship*) and an edited book on the impact of 9–11 and worldwide trauma on the providers of clinical care (*Terrorism and the Psychoanalytic Space: International Perspectives from Ground Zero*). Dr Cancelmo is a graduate of IPTAR's Adult Psychoanalytic Training Program and a graduate of the IPTAR Socio-Organizational Training Program in Organizational Consultation and Executive Coaching.

Paula L. Ellman, PhD, ABPP, FIPA, is a training and supervising analyst in the New York Freudian Society (NYFS) and the IPA. She is director of training of the New York Freudian Society and Washington DC Psychoanalytic Institute and a member of their permanent faculty. She is a board member of the Confederation of Independent Psychoanalytic Societies (CIPS). She has written and presented in the areas of female development, analytic listening, enactment, 9/11 terror, culture and psychoanalysis, and sadomasochism. She is co-editor (with Harriet Basseches and Nancy Goodman) of *Battling the Life and Death Forces of Sadomasochism: Theoretical and Clinical Perspectives* (Karnac, 2012). She has a private practice in psychotherapy and psychoanalysis in North Bethesda, Maryland and Washington, DC.

Allan Frosch, PhD, FIPA, is a training analyst and supervisor at the Institute for Psychoanalytic Research and Training (IPTAR) where he is also on the faculty. He is the author of a number of psychoanalytic articles and is twice past president of IPTAR, former dean of training, and former co-director of the IPTAR Clinical Center. Dr Frosch is also on the faculty at the Institute for Psychoanalytic Education (NYU Medical Center).

Nancy R. Goodman, PhD, FIPA, is a supervising and training analyst with the New York Freudian Society and the IPA. She has written papers and published in the areas of female development, analytic listening, Holocaust trauma and witnessing, film and psychoanalysis, 9/11 terror, the study of enactments, and sadomasochism. She is co-editor with Marilyn Meyers of a forthcoming volume: *The Power of Witnessing: Reflections, Reverberations, and Traces of the Holocaust* (Routledge, 2012). The book presents ideas about trauma and the way witnessing creates a living surround where symbolising can take place. It contains contributions by survivors, psychoanalysts, and scholars. Dr Goodman was director of training at the Washington DC Training Institute of the NYFS and is a member of the permanent faculty. She is chair of a teleconference group on enactment for CIPS, and has a full time psychoanalytic practice in Bethesda, MD.

Laurence J. Gould, PhD, FIPA, was a former director and professor of psychology in the Clinical Psychology Doctoral Program at the City University of New York. He was also a visiting professor and the founding co-director of the Program in Organizational Development and Consultation at Tel Aviv University, the founding editor of the journal *Organisational & Social Dynamics*, the director of the Socio-Analytic Training Program in Organizational Consultation and Executive Coaching at the Institute for Psychoanalytic Training and Research (IPTAR), and was the recipient of the American Psychological Association's Levinson Award for outstanding contributions to the theory and practice of organisational consultation. Dr. Gould had a private practice of psychoanalysis and organisational consultation in New York City.

Caron E. Harrang, LICSW, FIPA, is a clinical social worker and psychoanalyst working with infants, adolescents, and adults in Seattle, Washington. She teaches infant observation at the Northwestern Psychoanalytic Society. Caron has written on parent-infant psychotherapy, the relationship of aggression to original thought, and other topics related to psychoanalytic process and technique.

Richard Lasky, PhD, ABPP, FIPA, is associate dean and fellow at the Institute for Psychoanalytic Training and Research. He is clinical professor, training and supervising analyst, New York University Postdoctoral Program in Psychoanalysis and Psychotherapy. He is clinical and research associate and supervisor of psychotherapy, PhD Program in Clinical Psychology, City University of New York, and supervisor of psychotherapy, PsyD Program in Clinical and School Psychology, Pace University, New York.

Janice Lieberman, PhD, FIPA, is a psychoanalyst in private practice in New York. She is a faculty member and training and supervising analyst at the Institute for Psychoanalytic Training and Research, where she is the program chair and on the board of directors. She is also a member of the Psychoanalytic Association of New York (PANY). Dr Lieberman is the author of *Body Talk: Looking and Being Looked at in Psychotherapy* (2000) and co-author of *The Many Faces of Deceit: Omissions, Lies and Disguise in Psychotherapy* (1996), both published by Jason Aronson, as well as numerous articles about deception, gender, and contemporary art. She has been on the editorial boards of the *Journal of the American Psychoanalytic Association*, *The American Psychoanalyst*, and the *PANY Bulletin*. Currently she is North American chair of the IPA Public Information Committee. She has been a lecturer at the Whitney Museum of American Art for twenty years.

SERIES EDITOR'S PREFACE

Fredric T. Perlman, PhD, FIPA

I am honoured and also moved to introduce *Absolute Truth and Unbearable Psychic Pain: Psychoanalytic Perspectives on Concrete Experience*. This volume, the fifth instalment of the CIPS Book Series on the Boundaries of Psychoanalysis, offers a wealth of original contributions, all promising steps towards a fuller understanding of the phenomenon of "concreteness" and towards more effective approaches to the clinical challenges concreteness poses.

The terms "concrete thinking" and "concreteness" have more than one meaning in the professional literature, and are sometimes utilised to describe the incapacity to form higher-order concepts, categories, and abstractions from experience or, in some cases, the literal understanding of abstractions or metaphors. The essays comprising this volume address a different phenomenon, one that appears across a spectrum of diagnostic and clinical contexts and often underlies diverse clinical manifestations such as impulsivity, enactments, intractable transferences, bodily preoccupations, and the general fixity of the patient's representational world. Each of these clinical phenomena is discussed in one or more of the papers herein. In each of these clinical situations (and others like it), the patient unconsciously assigns a fixed meaning to persons and events, including the analyst and the analytic relationship, which is, for the patient, obvious and self-evident. These assigned meanings, which are dynamically determined and serve compelling psychological needs, nullify the possibility of any other meanings. The patient's ideas and feelings are thus experienced, not as products of complex mental activity (which includes but is not limited to perception), but as facts of life: inescapable, fundamental, and absolutely true.

In the grip of these convictions, the patient is trapped by his or her own construals in a narrow universe that squashes the potential for reflective deliberation and creative adaptation to life situations. At the same time, the analyst is similarly trapped. Any effort to interpret the patient's reality as a construction, forged of fact and fantasy, and shaped by forces beyond the patient's immediate grasp are, naturally enough, apt to appear to the patient as foolish or superfluous (at best) and as hostile, destructive, or crazy (at worst). Persistent efforts at interpretation are likely to eventuate in apparently unproductive conflicts between patient and analyst about "reality".

In some patients, concrete thought is restricted to certain sensitive areas of psychological concern, allowing a more or less normal analysis to proceed in other areas. But this is not always so. When such absolute certainty is pervasive, it may be understood as a character defence, strategically deployed to maintain a fixed phenomenal world, and aimed not at a particular set of contents, but rather at the core act of psychoanalysis itself: the interpretation of latent meanings. It will be seen that concreteness can pose a problem in any analysis, though the dimensions and specific features of this challenge will differ from patient to patient, as will the clinical approach that best promotes the psychological distance or "space" the patient needs in order to reflect upon his or her experience.

The papers that follow are all individual efforts but, as Thomas Kuhns, Ludwik Fleck, and many others have observed, no scientist or theoretician develops his or her ideas in isolation: every contributor is part of a scientific or professional community, a "thought collective", to use Fleck's evocative term. It will be evident that the authors of these papers are steeped in different psychoanalytic traditions. It may not be equally evident, however, that the authors of these papers are all part of a single but theoretically diverse psychoanalytic community that has been addressing selected clinical and theoretical issues, including the issue of concreteness, for the last twenty years. I am referring here to the CIPS community, a group of four psychoanalytic societies based in New York, Los Angeles, and Seattle, with individual members in New York, the District of Columbia, and elsewhere across the country.

Over its history, CIPS has celebrated its theoretical diversity while simultaneously endeavouring to make that diversity productive through clinical conferences, ongoing seminars, and more recently, by establishing this book series. In recent years, CIPS has held two clinical conferences, one on the topic of enactments and another on related topics of concreteness. These events, and the two book projects which they inspired (the current and upcoming volumes of the series), reflect the vibrant intellectual culture of the CIPS community.

Many people have contributed to this culture and this book series. Meg Beaudoin, the founding editor of the series, worked tirelessly to forge the right relationship with the right publisher, to bring together a team of editors, and to inspire our members to band together to develop book projects that reflect the work of our community. Steven J. Ellman has contributed enormously to our community dialogue by offering us a comprehensive review and integrative analysis of contemporary psychoanalysis in his book, *When Theories Touch,* the introductory volume in this series. The editors of each of the succeeding books in this series (Chris Christian, Michael Diamond, Andrew Druck, Carolyn Ellman, Norbert Freedman, Allan Frosch, Jesse Geller, Joan Hoffenberg, Marvin Hurvich, Aaron Thaler, and Rhonda Ward) as well as all the authors who have contributed so generously to these volumes have each advanced our thinking, our culture, and our sense of collective purpose.

Love, grief, and realism all converge to bring Bert Freedman to mind as I contemplate the growth and development of the CIPS community. Norbert Freedman, who died on November 30, 2011, was a towering figure in the IPTAR and CIPS communities, an analyst of rare erudition, creativity, and insightfulness whose contributions to psychoanalysis and to the organisational life of both IPTAR and CIPS are beyond calculation. My grief, and perhaps our collective grief, at his loss may be soothed by the knowledge that this book series, now publishing its fifth volume, is one of the many fruits whose seeds were first planted by Bert. It was Bert who first proposed the creation of the CIPS book series, predicting that a book series of our own would stimulate creativity, productivity, and new patterns of collegiality within our community. Those who are familiar with Bert's scholarly work will also be moved, as I am, to observe that the papers in this book reflect and advance Bert's pioneering work on the subject of concreteness and its opposite, reflective thought, insight, and integration, all of which Bert referred to as "symbolization". Virtually every author represented herein was influenced by Bert's ideas, either directly or indirectly, as evidenced by the frequent references to his work in these papers. Readers whose interest in Bert's work is piqued by this volume are referred to Volume Three of this series, *Another Kind of Evidence*, inspired and animated by Bert's creative ideas and his devotion to research, to the works cited in the bibliographies of these papers, and finally, to the exceptional volume published in his honour ten years ago, edited by his close colleague Richard Lasky, entitled *Symbolization and De-symbolization* (Other Press, 2002).

In April 2012, the IPTAR Board of Directors voted to celebrate Bert's life and legacy by establishing the Norbert Freedman Center for Psychoanalytic Research to honour his name and continue his work.

INTRODUCTION[1]

Allan Frosch

Abstract or conceptual thought is so much a part of our daily lives that, more often than not, we become acutely aware of it in its absence. Harold Searles (1962) brings this to our attention when he says to one of his patients, "It's just not in the cards for you, is it?" The patient responds to the metaphor by saying "I'm not playing cards," (p. 27). The literalness of the response can take us aback. This breakdown in metaphorical thinking is one form of what we call "concrete".

Concreteness, or what many refer to as desymbolised thinking/ experience (Freedman, 1997, 1998; Freedman & Lavender, 2002; Searles, 1962) or thing-presentations (Freud, 1915), reduces complexity. Things are what they are! There are no other possibilities. Concreteness takes many forms, can be intermittent or persistent and, depending on our theoretical orientation, has different aetiological contexts that predispose analysts to take diverse technical positions in their clinical work. The contributors to this volume come from a variety of theoretical/ clinical perspectives and their work highlights the protean nature of our subject.

In this introduction I try to articulate what I think may be a common thread in the diverse approaches whereby we attempt to help people transform the world of the concrete to the world of abstraction.

In my effort to do this, I will use different terms or theory-based constructs to refer to the same thing. In using theoretically different but functionally equivalent concepts, I am responding to the richness of psychoanalytic pluralism that encourages us to look at things from multiple perspectives.

In this paper the term "symbolisation" (or abstraction) refers to a process whereby we can meaningfully understand that an event can be looked at from a variety of perspectives. Symbolisation makes it possible to look at things in an "as if" way rather than as "true" or absolute. It is a process where we can view our thoughts as objects of our thoughts (Flavell, 1963). We self-reflect. Furthermore, it is a term that always includes its counterpart: desymbolisation (concreteness), where things are what they appear to be (Frosch, 2006). In the language of metapsychology, the abstract and concrete correspond to "word-presentations" and "thing-presentations" (Freud, 1915). Thing-presentations operate according to the laws of the primary process. They are unconscious, absolute, driven, and have a "perceptual identity" like the hallucination of the breast for a hungry baby. Word-presentation, or thought identity, is a secondary process activity that stands for/symbolises the unconscious thing-presentations. Here language is seen as a necessary part of a process of transforming primary process to secondary process organisation so that people can play with ideas, i.e., follow different paths between ideas without being led astray by the intensity of those ideas (Freud, 1900, p. 602; Laplanche & Pontalis, 1973, pp. 305–306). With this transformation we are no longer in the grip of compulsive adherence to the unconscious fantasies, i.e., thing-presentations. Words, however, while necessary, are not sufficient. The words of the analyst must take place in a particular emotional context.

I believe the analyst's capacity to regress to more primary process levels of organisation and then to re-establish his/her own level of symbolisation or secondary process activity is the central organising theme of our clinical work with all patients but, in particular, with those patients whose worlds are split into discrete bits of "reality" defined by the immediacy of experience. That is to say, those patients organised on a primary process "thing-presentation" or desymbolised level. This movement between primary and secondary process, between the concrete and the abstract, must take place in a libidinally charged emotional atmosphere in order for thing-presentations to be connected to word-presentations in a meaningful way. The libidinal investment, like the movement along the continuum of desymbolisation and symbolisation must be bidirectional. Although I believe each member of the analytic dyad helps the other in this fluidic process (Frosch, 2006), it is the analyst who must take the lead in the initiation and maintenance of this analytic milieu.

Psychoanalysis and concreteness

If the capacity for symbolisation is a basic requirement for social discourse (Searles, 1962) we can easily understand why the "concrete patient" is often considered *persona non grata* as a candidate for psychoanalysis. This exclusionary attitude is not limited to people who have difficulty with abstract (or conceptual) thinking and experience. It seems to be a tradition in our profession—although one best honoured by its breach—to exclude from analytic work people who make us uncomfortable. In this volume, however, we are focused on psychoanalytic perspectives of concrete experience and, in my opinion, it was Harold Searles as much, or more than anyone, who extricated the concrete patient from exclusion from the human race and from analytic treatment. He did this by making it crystal clear that the concrete thinking and experience we encounter in psychoanalysis is part of a dynamic process that he called "desymbolisation". Desymbolisation refers to a process where conceptual or abstract thought, secondary process thought, is now very literal or concrete so that once-attained metaphorical meanings have become "desymbolised" (Searles, 1962, p. 43). The impact of Searles's paper cannot be overestimated. He laid out the conceptual terrain for future generations of analysts to explore (see Lasky, 2002).

Concreteness and complexity

Concreteness is a topic that has been denigrated because it is both poorly understood and, most importantly, because it makes us as people and analysts so uncomfortable. As Searles says, we tend to look at the concrete person as alien, not part of the human race. The very title of this volume, *Absolute Truth and Unbearable Psychic Pain: Psychoanalytic Perspectives on Concrete Experience*, includes a variety of perspectives on how we view desymbolisation as a way of coping with psychic pain; but I think it is most likely the defensive function that we think about.

And this has been a major emphasis in the literature, but not an exclusive one at all (see Frosch, 1998; Grand, 2002; Schimek, 2002).

My own approach to this subject is to view concrete or desymbolised experience as a compromise formation driven by psychic pain. Like all compromise formations it has a defensive function as well as express-ing libidinal and aggressive wishes. As analysts we tend to highlight its maladaptive aspect although a more even-handed approach that also highlights certain adaptive aspects is necessary for a more complete understanding of the concept. Consider the following vignette pre-sented by Dr Stefano Bolognini (IPTAR, 16 January 2011):

> In her first analytic session a woman in her mid-twenties presents a dream rich in religious and sexual imagery. As she begins to associ-ate to the dream, she stops and asks the analyst whether he would prefer to be paid in cash or by cheque.

In the context of this volume, this is a very clear example of the movement from the metaphorical to the concrete serving a defensive function. The patient seems to move away from the passionate imagery of the dream to the more prosaic topic of the business arrangements of the relationship. As analysts we know, however, that money is rarely, if ever, a passionless issue; and Dr Bolognini tells us that the issue of money came to play a significant role in the transference. The patient wanted to be the analyst's special child and be treated free of charge. So her movement from the abstract to the concrete also allows this patient to express an inchoate transference wish; and it provides the analyst with an opportunity to have some sense of the unconscious fan-tasies as they present in early derivative form.

When we embrace the notion that the "the concrete" is another piece of complex analytic material, we can bring our psychoanalytic explo-ration of concrete experience into a more encompassing domain that allows us to look at things from multiple perspectives; but not all the time. When we are riddled with unpleasure (e.g., anxiety or some form of depressive affect) we can all narrow things down to one point of view. It is a point of view that reduces our emotional discomfort; and it is a point of view that stands alone. That is to say, it is not part of a world of ideas.

Searles (1962) puts it as follows: concrete thinking has a static, fatalis-tic quality, associated with severe psychopathology that sets the person "hopelessly apart from his fellow human beings" (p. 23). What Searles is referring to here is the schizophrenic patient being stuck in a world where things are what they seem—absolute truth. In the world of the concrete, there is no differentiation between inside and outside, between thought and actuality, between self and other. Thoughts and emotions have a "thing" quality that is absolute. There is no *other*, no *other* perspective. "Rarely indeed, in these writings, is there any intimation that the therapist can have the rewarding, and even exciting, experience of seeing a schizophrenic patient become free from the chains of concrete—that is, undifferentiated—thinking, able now to converse with his fellow human beings" (1962, p. 27). In this scenario, of course, Searles brings in the clinician's countertransference. In other words, the therapist/analyst may also be stuck in a static, fatalistic world vis-a-vis the patient: "I found him [the same patient as above] maddeningly and discouragingly unable to deal with any comments which I couched in figurative terms. When, for example, antagonised by his self-righteous demandingness, I told him abruptly, you can't have your cake and eat it, too!, I felt completely helpless when he responded to this at a literal, concrete level, by saying, I don't want to eat any cake in this hospital! You can eat cake here, if you want to; I don't want to eat any cake here" (1962, p. 26).

In this vignette Searles shows us how the analyst's emotional state (antagonised by his self-righteous demandingness ... told him abruptly) is a trigger to the patient's "failure" to understand the metaphor. While this kind of concreteness is not typically seen in an outpatient practice of most analysts, nor do most analysts treat schizophrenic patients, Searles makes it clear "that there is an essential continuity in all symbolic functions, the psychodynamics to be described here possess relevance to other kinds of symbolization than metaphorical thinking alone" (1962, p. 23). I would add to this that the ideas contained in Searles's paper need not be confined to the schizophrenic patient. For example, a non-schizophrenic patient said to me: "My life has always been this way and will always be this way; and there is nothing you can tell me that I haven't thought of already." In other words, "There is no inner world that I can understand so that my life can be better; and there is no difference between us." I think this example is probably fairly common and easily identifiable by most analysts. What is also identifiable, but not necessarily in the clinical moment, is the analyst's input into an enactment. Clearly, this is not peculiar to Searles or to work with a particular kind of patient. My own experience (Frosch, 2002, esp. pp. 622–629) is that the analyst's discomfort is an important catalyst for these enactments; and concrete patients often make us very uncomfortable.

The pre-Oedipal world of concrete patients is a world of great intensity. It is alive in a very particular way. It certainly may not be pleasurable in the ways that we ordinarily think of pleasure. But it is passionate and action-oriented. More often than not the passion does not have a libidinal quality but is more organised around aggression. This link to the perversions (Bass, 1997) highlights a world of part objects, driven by the immediacy of the moment. The consensual world of "reality" pales in comparison to this fantasy world (see Steingart, 1983), driven by sensation and infused with wishes that reign supreme. What we ordinarily call "emotion" is qualitatively different in this anal/paranoid-schizoid world. Emotions have a primary process "thing" quality, feel all powerful, and are inexorably linked to action (Frosch, 1995, p. 432).

The world that I am describing exists to a greater or lesser extent for everyone. We can all think of myriad examples in our own lives—just consider the battles and attendant feelings on an organisational level in the world of psychoanalysis, or at your own institute. We can certainly identify such feeling states in the patients we work with. For some, this world is intermittent and represents a regressive alteration in ego functioning; for others it has, as Searles put it, more of a static quality. And on the world's stage, assassinations are done by people who unequivocally believe that only through a direct expression of aggression to another can their own lives have any meaning. The "rightness" of their cause is absolute. And when as analysts we feel that the rightness of our cause (our interpretation) is clear and we are passionate in our conviction, we might consider that we can be setting the stage for an enactment. It is customary to say that certain kinds of patients "induce" us into an enactment. Cause and effect become organised from our subjective perspective, and we label as accurate and absolute what, in retrospect, may be our countertransference. Arnold Rothstein talks about the analyst's love for his patient as the analyst trying to work through his/her countertransference (1999); and Hans Loewald (1960) talks about the analyst's resistance in a similar way.

Thing-presentations and word-presentations

In this section of the paper I will outline some of Loewald's (1960, 1970, 1980) thinking that allowed him to bring the metapsychology of psychoanalysis—"the hypercathexis of word and thing presentations" (Freud, 1915)—into the world of an emotionally charged relationship between analyst and patient where each is affected by the other. Loewald's work addresses the question of how we understand the transformation of a patient's desymbolised or unsymbolised experience, i.e., experience/mentation that is regressed, or has never attained secondary status. Loewald's answer to this is the same as Freud's: there must be a "hypercathexis" of word and thing presentation to "bring about a higher psychical organisation and make it possible for the primary process to be succeeded by the secondary process" (Freud, 1915, p. 202). In his discussion Loewald moves hypercathexis from a purely energic term to a transformational concept that takes place in a libidinised reciprocal psychic field (1970, pp. 64–65). Loewald is very much aware of the impact of his words: "While this may sound unfamiliar and perhaps too fanciful, it is only an elaboration, in nontechnical terms, of Freud's deepest thoughts ..." (1970, p. 65).

For Loewald defence—and here he is talking about repression—is "understood as an unlinking" (1980, p. 188) between thing and word presentations. The link between symbol and that which is symbolised (word and thing presentations) is repressed, i.e., severed or loosened; and the act of hypercathexis re-establishes the link (1980, pp. 183, 188). The analytic task involves (and here we can say this in a number of ways), e.g., 1) making the unconscious conscious, 2) transforming experience-bound and action-oriented unconscious things to "mental representations that stand for the experience" (Lasky, 1993, p. 260n.), or 3) bringing the primary process under the domain of secondary process organisation. The language we use to describe this process differs depending on our theoretical orientation. Whatever terminology we use, however, the process of transforming things to words is life-altering. It is a new way of ordering the world and allows the person to make inferences about an event that go beyond the immediately observable experience (Bruner, Goodnow & Austin, 1956). And the analyst does this through the use of words, i.e., interpretation. Even if we leave aside what we mean by "interpretation", there are a number of points to be made about this statement that bear directly on our understanding of the analytic process in general and, in particular, on how we understand the notion of concreteness.

Love and miracles

The interpretive work that links primary process things and secondary process words represents a link between analyst and patient. And this is Loewald's "novel" (1970, p. 68) approach to the concept of hyper-cathexis. "Hypercathexis, I believe, cannot be adequately understood if we fail to take into account that it originates within a supraindividual psychic field. Expressed in traditional psychoanalytic terms, the essential factor is that cathected objects are themselves cathecting agents. The subject which cathects objects is at the same time being cathected by those objects ..." (1970, p. 63). The mother—infant/child relationship and the analyst–analysand relationship:

> Are relations between mutually cathecting agents, and the cathecting of each partner is a function of the other's cathecting ... The higher-order cathecting activity of his libidinal objects (parents) constitutes, as it were, the first hypercathexis. In so far as the objects' cathecting operations are on secondary process levels (although they are by no means exclusively so), they have the potential of hypercathexes in terms of the subject's psychic processes. (1970, p. 63)

In the therapeutic situation it is the analyst "[who] helps to bring this about ... the analyst, mediates this union ... a new version of the way in which transformation of primary into secondary processes opened up in childhood, through mediation of higher organisation by way of early object-relations (1960, p. 31)." And Loewald makes it clear that in order to immerse himself in the patient's world, the analyst "must be able to regress within himself to the level of organization on which the patient is stuck ..." (1960, p. 26). The analyst, like the good-enough parent, must also be able to return to a more secondary process mode of functioning.

And all of this occurs in the context of love. For Loewald the analytic relationship is based on love and respect for the patient and the patient's love for the analyst. Just as it is impossible to have an analysis without loving the patient (1970, p. 65), it is impossible to have an analysis without the patient's love for the analyst. We can put all of this into the language of libidinal investments or transference/countertransference.

In doing this we communicate to our colleagues and ourselves that the love we are talking about falls within the "scientific", the "analytic", domain. We do not want to be misunderstood, and Loewald is acutely aware of the potential impact of his words: "In many quarters there still seems to be a tendency to put up a 'no admittance' sign when metapsychological considerations point to object relations as being not merely regulative *but essential constitutive factors in psychic structure formation*" (1970, p. 66, my emphasis). In the words of the poet, when we make an emotional (i.e., libidinal) investment in another person, "that person seems at once to belong to a different universe, is surrounded with poetry, (and) makes of one's life a sort of stirring arena ..." (Proust, 1913, p. 334). It is in this stirring arena of the analytic situation that the words of the analyst can take on a special meaning, a meaning that leads to an internalisation of a differentiated relationship that increases "the hypercathectic resources of the individual" (1970, p. 63).

It is this emotional atmosphere, this hypercathexis of self and other, that Freud was talking about when he said that the words of the analyst have the power to create "miraculous cures" (1905a, p. 289). It is easy enough to write off Freud's comments as hyperbole, as the overly optimistic words of someone embarking on a path of great discovery. While this may well be the case, consider for a moment the patient that Searles discussed who was so concrete. This patient, Searles tells us, "after five years of work ... can communicate confidently, with rare exceptions, in metaphorical as well as literal terms, seeing both levels of meanings in his own comments and in mine" (1962, p. 30). This seems like quite a miraculous accomplishment.

Passionate abstractions

Although Freud's language in the 1905 paper is very far from the metapsychology of energy transformations, his ideas in this paper are consistent with his own metapsychological abstractions in 1915 as well as Loewald's use of metapsychology. In the 1905 paper Freud presents, in the concrete immediacy of experience, the underpinnings of his energic abstractions. When Freud talks about the rapport between analyst and patient and likens it to the relationship between a mother and her infant (1905a, p. 295), he begins to tell us about the bidirectional passion and intensity of the analytic relationship.

Freud says quite directly that the analyst helps to create an expectation of faith and hope in his patient that lends a certain magic to the analyst's words (1905a, p. 291). And it is the analyst's interest that potentiates this "propitious state" of mind in the patient (p. 293). And, I would add, it is not an interest that can be understood in purely intellectual or cerebral terms. In English the word "interest" refers to the relation of being objectively concerned in something. In the German (*Interesse*), there is more of a sense of personal involvement. It is related to a very common phrase (*im stiche lassen*), "to leave in the lurch" (cf. Freud, 1910, p. 12); thus "one's interest or personal involvement with a patient allows us to enter most profoundly into the core of the patient's life—or soul" (*Seele*, 1905a, p. 283n.; 1905b, p. 254). Without this interest/involvement we are left out in the lurch.

Freud's language conveys a very personal connection and repulsion that speaks directly to the passions of the analytic relationship. In the complex and highly charged analytic situation the reciprocal relationship between expectations based on hope and faith and the analyst's interest argues against linear statements of cause and effect, so that interest and expectation are co-constructed or subject and object are hypercathected. This kind of process has been described by Bach (2006) who likens the analyst's attention to his patient as a kind of secular prayer with curative value in its own right.

Concluding comments

It is in this emotional context that we can best understand Loewald's thinking that the analyst's interpretive activity gives rise to a new mental representation: "an intrapsychic perception induced by the words of the analyst that may be conscious but in *all likelihood may occur outside of consciousness*" (1980, p. 183). I emphasise the latter part of Loewald's statement because it resonates so well with much of our current psychoanalytic outcome research that highlights the central importance of the internalisation (largely unconscious—see Falkenstrom, Grant, Broberg & Sandell, 2007, p. 666) of the differentiated relationship with the analyst for long-term therapeutic gain (Frosch, 2011). I believe this is what Loewald means when he talks about increasing the patient's resources for hypercathexis. I understand this as an increased capacity to [re]-establish a link between the thing and the word so that the concrete can enter into the world of abstraction.

But Loewald has more to say about interpretation and the transformation of the concrete to the abstract. It is not simply establishing or re-establishing a connection between the unconscious fantasy (thing-presentation) and the consciously (Loewald refers to it as preconscious) perceived object (word-presentation). There must be an optimal linking. Mental functioning is seen as a compromise between a too intimate and intense closeness to the unconscious (with its "creative and destructive aspects", 1980, p. 189) and a less than adequate libidinal link between word and thing so that language has a "hollow quality … no longer vibrant and warmed by the 'fire' of the unconscious" (p. 189). In the first instance the unconscious fantasy replaces reality and we are in the world of things—the concrete. In the second instance language is meaningless and the consensual world of reality loses any significance. These are two aspects of the same multidimensional continuum differentially emphasised by the authors in this volume depending on their theoretical orientation and clinical technique. In the chapters that follow, the abstractions of thing presentations and word presentations in a hypercathected psychic field are replaced with the concrete immediacy of the relationship between analyst and patient as they work to transform absolute beliefs into ideas that stand in relation to other ideas.

References

Bach, S. (2006). *Getting from Here to There: Analytic Love, Analytic Process*. Hillsdale, NJ: The Analytic Press.

Bass, A. (1997). The problem of "concreteness". *Psychoanalytic Quarterly, 66*: 642–682.

Bolognini, S. (2011). A session with Antonia. Presentation at IPTAR.

Bruner, J. S., Goodnow, J. L. & Austin, G. A. (1956). *A Study of Thinking*. New York: Wiley.

Flavell, J. H. (1963). *The Developmental Psychology of Jean Piaget*. Princeton, NJ: Van Nostrand.

Freedman, N. (1997). On receiving the patient's transference: The symbolizing and desymbolizing countertransference. *Journal of the American Psychoanalytic Association, 45*: 79–103.

Freedman, N. (1998). Psychoanalysis and symbolization: Legacy or heresy? In: C. Ellman, S. Grand, M. Silvan & S. Ellman (Eds.), *The Modern Freudians: Contemporary Psychoanalytic Technique* (pp. 79–97). Northvale, NJ: Jason Aronson.

Freedman, N. & Lavender, J. (2002). On desymbolization: The concept and observations on anorexia and bulimia. *Psychoanalysis and Contemporary Thought*, 25: 165–199.

Freedman, N., Lasky, R. & Ward, R. (2009). The upward slope: A study of psychoanalytic transformations. *Psychoanalytic Quarterly*, 78: 201–231.

Freud, S. (1900). *The Interpretation of Dreams. S. E., 5*. London: Hogarth.

Freud, S. (1905a). Psychical (or mental) treatment. *S. E., 7*. London: Hogarth.

Freud, S. (1905b). Freud's psycho-analytic procedure. *S. E., 7*. London: Hogarth.

Freud, S. (1910). Five lectures on psycho-analysis. *S. E., 11*. London: Hogarth.

Freud, S. (1915). The unconscious. *S. E., 14*. London: Hogarth.

Frosch, A. (1995). The preconceptual organization of emotion. *Journal of the American Psychoanalytic Association*, 43: 423–447.

Frosch, A. (1998). Narcissistic injury and sadomasochistic compensation in a latency-age boy. In: P. Beren (Ed.), *Narcissistic Disorders in Children and Adolescents: Diagnosis and Treatment* (pp. 263–280). Northvale, NJ: Jason Aronson.

Frosch, A. (2002). Transference: Psychic reality and material reality. *Psychoanalytic Psychology*, 19: 603–633.

Frosch, A. (2006). Analyzability. *Psychoanalytic Review*, 93: 835–843.

Frosch, A. (2011). The effect of frequency and duration on psychoanalytic outcome: A moment in time. *Psychoanalytic Review*, 98: 11–38.

Laplanche, J., Pontalis, J.-B. (1973). *The Language of Psychoanalysis*. New York: W. W. Norton.

Lasky, R. (1993). *Dynamics of Development and the Therapeutic Process*. Northvale, NJ: Jason Aronson.

Lasky, R. (Ed.) (2002). *Symbolization and Desymbolization: Essays in Honor of Norbert Freedman*. New York: Other Press.

Loewald, H. W. (1960). On the therapeutic action of psycho-analysis. *International Journal of Psychoanalysis*, 41: 16–33.

Loewald, H. W. (1970). Psychoanalytic theory and the psychoanalytic process. *Psychoanalytic Study of the Child*, 25: 45–68.

Loewald, H. (1980). Primary process, secondary process, and language (1978). In: *Papers on Psychoanalysis* (pp. 178–206). New Haven, CT: Yale University Press.

Proust, M. (1913). *In Search of Lost Time, Volume 1, Swann's Way*. New York: The Modern Library, 2003.

Rothstein, A. (1999). Some implications of the analyst feeling disturbed while working with disturbed patients. *Psychoanalytic Quarterly*, 68: 541–558.

Searles, H. F. (1962). The differentiation between concrete and metaphorical thinking in the recovering schizophrenic patient. *Journal of the American Psychoanalytic Association*, 10: 22–49.
Steingart, I. (1983). *Pathological Play in Borderline and Narcissistic Personalities*. Jamaica, NY: Spectrum.

Note

1. My thanks to Dr William Fried, Batya Monder, and Ruth Oscharoff for their input during the preparation of this paper.

CHAPTER ONE

Concretisation, reflective thought, and the emissary function of the dream

Maxine Anderson

Introduction

It seems that we live in at least two mental worlds: one defined by intense sensory experience, and another more gently crafted by attunement and thought. While we may wish to think of ourselves as residing primarily and maturely amid thought and reflection, a clear-eyed view will reveal that we spend much if not most of our time in the concrete, sensory-dominated world of "how it is". Indeed this sensory level of experience shades and shapes much of the texture of our emotional lives, but perhaps due to its bedrock nature and profound impact, it may also exert a gravitational pull, easily dismantling the products of thought and our capacities to think back into the basic sensory elements from which they evolve. In this chapter I will attempt to explore some aspects of this to and fro between these two realms of the psyche and the de-animating power of the entropic pull. In addition I will illustrate some countermeasures we may employ to restore and protect the realm of thought. And I will also suggest that the well-attended dream has a role to play both as guide to and emissary between these different realms of the psyche.

1

One added introductory note: while heavily influenced by Bion, and several of his students, whom I will note, I will try to remain descriptive of clinical and personal experience in this discussion, hoping to invite new ideas to emerge and to avoid the possible narrowing of thought which heavy reliance upon theory can impose.

The concrete state of mind

Simply put, the concrete state of mind relates to reality in terms of sensory perception and sensory experience, defining reality in terms of what the peripheral senses convey. More specifically it is a state of mind in which metaphor and symbolic thought are not available. For instance, before the laws of gravity came into general awareness, people explained apples dropping from a tree as "just falling down". Without access to symbolic thought or reasoning we rely on sensory experience and sensory-based explanations of reality.

From this perspective there is no reference to interiority or to inner space where one may feel held in mind or where thought might reside. Years ago a five-year-old patient responded to my giving a thoughtful context for his rampages with a startled statement of "Oh, at my house we don't do that … things just happen and then Mom yells at me." This young patient was expressing the experiential world of "how it is" ("things just happen"), but once he felt held in mind by my efforts to understand he could begin to contrast this with his experience of his mother's non-receiving ("yelling") state of mind. At the time I was impressed by this very young child's observation, but also I could more deeply appreciate how a child's development including his capacities for thought may be impacted by his parent's (in)capacities to receive and to really think about his experiences and expressions.

The development of the capacity for thought

My current notions about the development of the capacity for reflective thought involve the notion of "reverie", Bion's notion of the quality of the care-taking mind's openness to respond to tension or distress, and by way of thinking about that distress to transform it into meaning (Bion, 1962). The distress-based self then gradually learns that a mind "out there" is transforming his/her unthinkable experience into meaningful communication. The growing self thus learns through the process of being thought about how to think about itself and the world. This capacity, born by feeling held in mind, offers a leap beyond the two-dimensional, concrete "how it is" world. A three-dimensional mind with space for thought and reflection comes into view via the experience of having been thought about, and having felt known. And it is this same function that serves our therapeutic efforts to nourish our distressed patients, as well as our own distressed selves. Nevertheless, when concretisation is predominant, we need to be aware that these thinking and knowing capacities will often collapse back to the two-dimensional ("how it is") mental world defined by sensory experience, often with such intensity as to be considered a so-called "truth".

The tension between two mental realms

Such a collapse into the concrete may occur more often than we might imagine, as evidenced by our powerful uncontained emotions. For example, when we are encumbered by fear, anxiety, or rage we feel pressured and defensive but also probably unable to conceptualise that we are being tormented by fear, pressured by anxiety, or swept away by rage. Our clamorous emotions so easily overtaking the quiet space of repose and thought reduce any sense of inner space to a two-dimensional, reactive experience etched by that affect. And when we cannot think about this process we are condemned to be defined by that sensory experience, so that we are unable to think about being tormented or pressured; instead, we feel concretely "trapped forever" within that fear, rage, or anxiety. A similar state is characteristic of our intensely held "certainties": in the absence of thought we are condemned to the pressured insistence of being either absolutely right, or catastrophically wrong.

The similarity continues, when as the clinician I feel I have become the target of an intense barrage, such as a penetrating accusation, or overwhelming rage, I may feel my boundaries thinned or breached, and feel myself inclined to slip into a concrete, reactive place as well. The barrage may be something my patient cannot bear to feel, such as a sense of futility, incompetence, or stupidity, which then is unconsciously but violently projected my way. In my clinical openness I may then feel that unbearable emotion, and because of the intensity of the projection I feel overtaken or defined by its "truth", and then in turn "become" the hopeless, incompetent, or stupid one. Of course, when so defined I do not have access to my thinking self, and am thus unable to think about the situation as a matter of my receiving and not being able to metabolise a mind-numbing projection. In order to reverse this process of concretisation, that is to rescue my thinking capacity, I need to be able to develop a sturdy boundary, in the moment, if possible, or continuously, as I can, in order to protect my thought and my capacity for awareness about the nature of this type of functioning. And, as most of us know, acquiring this facility often takes years of clinical experience.

Another circumstance related to my slipping into the concrete, reactive mode is my own inner debilitation, be it from fatigue, pre-occupation, chagrin, or any other of those elements that can trigger doubt about my own capacities. My own doubt can penetrate and wither my thinking capacities as thoroughly as can my patient's accusations, and can lead to my connection with my thinking self giving way to a heavy, dull sense of "being incompetent or stupid or wrong". It is as if doubt mimics the erosive effects of concretisation, acting to neutralise the products of thought, and altering meaning from an animate (thinkable) state toward a deanimated (drained of meaning or unthinkable) one. It follows here that when I am without thought I am condemned to concrete experience and reactivity.

Concretisation as the mechanism for the deanimation of thought

I would now like to turn to some of the mechanisms involved in this concretising process. In a previous paper (Anderson, 1999) I include a quote from P. C. Sandler (1997): "There appears to be a universal tendency to replace psychic reality with material reality, which coexists with and opposes the development of thinking … [that is] the existence of an active concretization … [which] 'turns' in phantasy, in the mind of the person, either patient or analyst, what is animate (linked with meaning) into what is inanimate (a more meaningless sensory state)" (p. 47).

In his argument for the concept of a normative concretising function which he terms "anti-alpha function", Sandler further states:

> The human mind has difficulty containing immaterial abstractions within psychic boundaries … The material products resulting from the action of anti-alpha function carry with them from the

beginning the marks of such defensive processes as denial, reaction formation, displacement and condensation. The concretization of psychic reality precludes the occurrence of free association ... [and fosters] acting out. When anti-alpha function is in operation, one is bound to "transform", as it were, energy into matter ... it seems that the mind promotes an active transformation of what is alive into what is dead, and people deal with living creatures and their productions ... as if they were inanimate ... the container or receptacle is also regarded as an inanimate thing. (1997, pp. 47–49)

As part of his discussion, Sandler also reviews the way concretisation fuels the virulence of some forms of projective identification:

Projective identification is the concretization of an emotion and of feelings; through this very concretization one is enabled to build up a phantasy of "projecting" something into someone else, for the "something" projected is not a thing, it is not material, but the person who projects deals with it sensuously, as if it were a concrete thing amenable to be projected ... (1997, p. 48).

Elsewhere in my paper I also mention Meltzer's notion that the vulnerable receiver of those projections also deals with them sensuously. When we do not have access to our protected thinking selves (our "good internal objects" to use Meltzer's terms) we are subject to being overwhelmed by the bombardment of untransformable sensory elements (withering projections or accusations) and thus to being defined by them ("becoming dull and incompetent") which—again in Meltzer's terms—is finding oneself encumbered by "dead objects". Meltzer holds that this is a universal human occurrence when live-minded thought is not available. Concretisation, then, may usefully be thought of as the mechanism active in the deanimation of thought or as providing the gateway where dead objects may enter or prevail (Anderson, 1999, p. 513).

The lack of inner agency and the pull to the familiar

The self in a sensory-dominated world, then, not in touch with the interiority of mindfulness, has no notion of mental space or of inner agency. Instead the self is experienced as a two-dimensional target or surface for sensory impact, and can only relate reactively to agency and responsibility as if to causes and powers residing outside the self ("It's all your fault" … "My boss is so mean and I am so small" or … "There is no help available"). And in this state without the protection of compassionate thought the cruel, self-battering so-called superego, as the embodiment of psychic trauma, is experienced concretely as a brutal, condemning "truth" about one's inadequacy or badness.

One patient, Ms A, lost her mother when she was very small, and due to an overwhelmed family atmosphere she seemed to have had little or no experience in feeling held in mind or known about. While she has attained moderate success professionally, she seems to have spent much of her life feeling lost or "in hiding", moderately and at times seriously depressed, paralysed by passivity, and unable to feel much sense of attachment or commitment to person or place. Loyalty to and identification with her dead mother appears to underlie a "bleak forever" state of mind, which early in our work seemed impervious to my attempts to bring understanding. While more recently she has come to feel more accompanied and understood—and thus more alive—this reprieve is short-lived as she seems to gravitate back to the identification with the inanimate bleakness as "who I am … what I have always known". It appears that loyalties to the familiar past, as deadened and painful as they may be, can powerfully outweigh the as yet unknown possibilities for new life and hope which my patient discovers when she can internalise our work and begin to connect with live-minded thought, attendant self-reflection, and budding self-respect.

Yet at times our patients do have rather clear insights into these burdensome dilemmas that can so entrap them: Mr B, subject to violent outbursts but also capable at times of reflecting upon his own concreteness, observed, I thought astutely, that his immaturities and agitations seem to propel him back into the state where his familiar violent primitive emotions take charge, convincing him that to invoke restraint and concern is "too hard … not fair … too much of a burden". Mr B seemed to eloquently express how the violent protest from his own concrete states could attack or expel potential thought and inner agency. He further seemed to be describing an outrage that creates a war zone, violently shredding his inner authority ("It's not fair … I shouldn't have to") such that at those times he feels caught in the debris field of jagged self-loathing ("I'm so worthless … just a piece of shit"). He continues to describe these attacks upon his own capacities as preserving a "perverse bubble" (his words) as a residence for the infantile, impulsive, impoverished self, which so hates (and so refuses) to grow up. These reflections, he muses, are an elaborate description of a complicated, self-perpetuating temper tantrum.

While Mr B cannot yet fully appreciate the development of his self-observing capacities, I can appreciate them and can also witness their continued growth even alongside the violent outbursts, which, while diminishing, can still wreak internal havoc. Meanwhile, these states of self-condemnation are heart-wrenching to witness because when the patient is in their grip he is entirely out of touch with any sense of history, hope, or the possibility for growth.

We can see then that what we consider as emotional growth is a complex business. The rather quiet forces for mental growth are countered by familiar and thus persuasive sensory intensities, which concretely press towards the status quo as "the truth" or "what I have always known". These resistances to change, because of their power and tenacity, seem to resemble a force of nature.

Working clinically with concrete mental states

I would now like to illustrate some aspects of the dilemma that emerges at the interface between concreteness and reflective thought, by way of a few clinical vignettes from my work with a patient I have seen for several years, a woman, whom I will call Ms C. This woman, the youngest of several children, felt exposed not only to the absence of an emotionally available mother but also to the presence of paternal cruelty, as well as to the consequence of family chaos, abuse, and neglect cascading from preceding generations. Such trauma and the absence of protective reverie have for much of her life left my patient feeling persecuted and identified with the chaos, ready to defend it as "freedom" in the face of any attempts to bring order or containment. Even so, she has struggled ceaselessly to get the therapeutic help she so desperately needs in order to grow. I think our mutual regard for the therapy and for each other bring resilience on both our parts to this often tempestuous work.

Technically, I find my attempts to speak therapeutically to her require ongoing care. For instance, when she is feeling tormented and chaotic any comment of mine is felt to be an attempt to restrain her, to limit her "freedom" and thus to force something upon her. I often have to speak to that very issue to demarcate the way she experiences my attempts to label and contain her chaos as "squelching her freedom". Also, since in this state of mind she perceives her literal experience to be the only possible view, any difference on my part is felt as my being at best "not understanding" but more likely as my causing her distress by my non-alignment. Here then, "understanding" is equated with "agreement" and any separate-mindedness is considered to be a cause for suspicion and blame. I therefore have to remain aware of this tension regarding non-alignment and at times speak to "how misunderstanding and per-haps even how mean you feel me to be when I do not agree with your point of view" or something similar.

In addition, as suggested, when Ms C is caught in a pit of hate and despair she feels defined by that brutal chaos of her childhood, and all my best efforts are likely to be seen through the lens of negativity. Recently I realised several hours before an appointment with her that I might be late in returning from an emergent appointment of my own away from the office. I felt that she would likely become very agitated if I was not there at the accustomed time, so I thought it wise for me to call and leave word that I might be a few minutes late. The only oppor-tunity I had to make this call, given the timing of the day, was just a couple of minutes before another patient came. I did manage to reach and inform Ms C, who seemed appreciative, but I then had to ring off as my next scheduled patient was ringing in. At the time I felt relieved to have reached her.

As it turned out I was not late, but when she came in several hours later she was in a rage, saying "Never call me again, never ... never ...." It took her several minutes to calm down and I could see that the call had deeply distressed her, which was at first puzzling to me. Over the hour I could piece together that she felt my possibly being late meant that I was preferring to be with someone other than her, and to make matters worse that I had rung off abruptly, probably to see that some-one else, an action which just rubbed her nose in the "fact" of my not preferring her. Ms C's outrage filled the room and nearly the whole of my mind as well, and it was difficult for me to think or say any-thing helpful; further, any potential understandings were only mocked and belittled. Feeling quite attacked I had to fight to keep a clear head; and any attempt to frame her rage in terms of her feeling so hurt was met with such disdain that at the time I only felt small and helpless. In addition I could feel myself nudging towards descent into a concrete retaliatory rage, a wish to throw up my hands and more or less yell back at her. But in my efforts to stay thoughtful about my patient, I recalled a dream we had looked at together in the previous hour, a dream whose clear understandings now seemed to offer something for me to hold onto:

> She and another woman are in the army and were about to go and see an explosion. She is terrified about the explosion, as if it could go off at any time. But the woman says she will go to a safe position to view the explosion and she, the patient, says she will go too, even though she feared that it might make her AWOL. She does go along with the woman and yet she feels guilty. After the explosion, which did not injure either of them, the patient thinks she may sneak back to pretend she had been there, at the site of the explosion all the time, so she won't be reported as AWOL.

The dream had been understood as the two of us being capable of witnessing her explosive rage safely, but that she also feels compelled by old rigid and adherent aspects which demand that she remain strong and loyal, that is not go AWOL, from that militant explosiveness. She seemed relieved by this understanding.

I was able to remind my still angry patient of this dream and some of our understandings, wondering aloud if they could help us sort out some of her current intense feeling. She seemed able to calm down and listen to me and to recall the dream and its potential meanings. Shortly thereafter, perhaps reconnecting with thought, she was able to admit that following the previous hour, perhaps because of the work we had done with the dream, she had become obsessed with the wish to possess me and all my capacities, and so that my needing to ring off in my call to her had been felt as my defying her possessive aims. In an instant she felt sure that I was wishing to get rid of her altogether, a jarring perception felt as a "certainty", which then triggered the current explosive rage. Carefully we were able to sort out that following the work on the explosion dream in the previous hour my patient's gratitude for the emerging understanding was overtaken by her greed to possess the source of that understanding; that the obsession to possess me was allowing the lust for power to overwhelm the gratitude and respect which our work had engendered. My patient's experience of my phone call reflected her intensely felt fantasy of my dispossessing her for her greed, preferring others, and rubbing salt into an old wound.

As we carefully found our way out of this morass I was reminded of how greed and envy can so degrade the realm of thought and gratitude into the concrete states defined by possession, power, and revenge. But I was also reminded how disturbing any change in the frame, such as my phone call, can be. And indeed, in the absence of reflective thought any alteration of the frame can only be viewed with suspicion if not the conviction of negative intent.

The dream as guide through concrete experience

On several occasions while working with concreteness and concretisation I have found the patient's dreams to be quite helpful. I find it my style to work actively with dreams and of course that encourages the patient to bring more dreams. From this way of working, I have found many instances in which the dreams seem to bypass the defensive, entrapped, concrete state of mind of the patient, and as it were to "speak" to the analyst as if pointing the way forward. For example, Ms C had a dream in which:

> She told a couple, who were asking for directions, how to reach their destination, by going up a hill and then turning right at the top of the hill. But after the couple left, she then turned around and without watching, she allowed herself to slip into a pool of green slime such that she nearly drowned.

She awoke in a panic, fearing that indeed she was about to drown in that slime.

Following her reporting the dream she complained of feeling tired and restless and did not want to think any more about it. After a bit I offered that the dream might be suggesting that in it she could point the way forward to the couple, our working dyad, indeed up a hill, probably hard work, but something attainable. But then the dream may also suggest that in the absence of the couple (that is, between our sessions) she seems to turn back to being neglectful of herself, easily slipping back into a drowning pool of self-neglect. Her dream, I continued, may be more wide awake than she could be at times, showing the way out of the mess she can so readily slip back into. This way of viewing the dream was of interest to my patient and we were able to utilise this message from the dream for some time.

An alternative view of the same dream, which came to light during discussion of this clinical material with colleagues (Princeton, NJ, March 19–21, 2010) was that between her therapy hours, when she imagined that I would be with others perhaps in an excited way (a couple going up the hill), she could easily lose touch with the strenuous work she and I have done, and collapse into self-neglect, slipping into a drowning pool of envy (green slime). Both of these readings of the dream pertain to the patient's deep issues and perhaps these readings of slightly varying relevance demonstrate the multi-faceted nature of the dream.

And another dream from Ms C, which has been of interest:

> She is on a fire escape and looking down to see her father and siblings on a landing, seemingly stuck. She feels great pity for them, and notices that, surprisingly, she can walk past them and continue on down the fire escape to safety, feeling sadness for them, but relief for herself.

As we initially tried to look at the dream she was again at first restless and wishing to find distraction from the dream. Having her tendency for self-neglect in mind, I then suggested she was having difficulty seeing clearly what the dream might be trying to show her in terms of her being able to gain safety and freedom from the fiery experience of her childhood family. While the path towards emergence was available, there was still a part of her that was reluctant to move past the traumatising family and to leave them on the fire escape.

Once my patient had a clear sense of this dream she was able to hold it in mind for several weeks, and we were both able to think of her reluctance to change which involved separating from her childhood family; it seemed that my being able to link with the clarity of the dream allowed her to do so as well. It is inviting to think that the dream itself was a fire escape of a sort, showing the path down to safety and to clear-eyed thought, which seemed to be the links needed to fully access that way forward.

Again, in discussion with the same colleagues the possibility that these dreams occurred sequentially was raised and we mused that such a sequence could be viewed as a chronicle of her potential development:

1. The explosion dream depicting her entrapment by or addiction to the traumatising chaos and abuse, but also expressing the possibility of gaining help in transforming this violence by way of our mutual work.
2. The dream about the couple and the green slime, representing her dependence upon the analyst and the work, while also subjecting it and herself to the ravages of self-neglect and envy.
3. And the fire escape dream, depicting the possibility of separating from the familiar chaos and abuse (leaving the family) while also beginning a process of mourning (feeling sad for the family) which such separation makes possible.

I offer these creative musings to illustrate both the kaleidoscopic nature of the dream and the evolving meanings possible among collaborative minds.

As I wrote these vignettes, while also appreciating the creative elaborations just mentioned, I recalled with awe the complexity of the dreaming process, its communicative potential, and the depth of the wisdom of the dream. In addition I came upon the recently published works of Jim Grotstein (2009) and Thomas Ogden (2009), both of whom review Bion's notions of dreaming and its profoundly important impact on the organisation and growth of the mind. As a counterpoint to Sandler's comment on an intrinsic deanimating process, "Bion is proposing that the human personality is constitutionally equipped with mental operations that generate personal symbolic meaning, consciousness, and the potential for unconscious psychological work with one's emotional problems" (Ogden, p. 103). Ogden further mentions that the dreaming function for Bion is synonymous with unconscious thinking, due in large part to its binocular capacity to view an emotional situation from both conscious and unconscious perspectives. Via this binocularity "dreaming is our profoundest form of thinking and constitutes the principal medium through which we achieve human consciousness, psychological growth, and the capacity to create personal, symbolic meaning from our lived experience" (Ogden, p. 104). My attending to my patient's dreams may have served to help her connect with the value of this binocularity, that is to gain access to the lessons from these dreams—her loyalty to the militant explosiveness, her hesitation to bypass her chaotic family on the landing—and to be able to think about rather than be enmeshed by these ancient concrete states of mind. My helping my patient to value the dream lessons may have aided her developing symbolic capacity, helpful in counteracting the deanimating pull of the self-neglect, the loyalty to the explosiveness, and her addiction to "chaos as freedom".

Even with the help of the dream, however, the way forward is not always this clear-cut: my patient is often caught in a place defined by the past, bound by its intense concrete "certainties". But she is also in dread of anything new, for that would involve uncertainty, which triggers dread of the unknown. While the dream might show a clear path forward (fire escape), my patient often seems to get caught on the landing with the old entangling internal family, unable and/or unwilling to move away from that dreaded familiarity towards the perhaps even more dreaded uncertain future. Such is the pull towards the ancient, the familiar, the unchanging which lends conviction to the simultaneous wish and dread that seem to shape "how it will always be".

The struggles of the analyst to metabolise concrete experience

In such stuck times I try to take care to refrain from collapsing into the impatient ("If I've told you once I've told you 1000 times ...") state of mind, which occurs at moments when I am feeling weary and thus susceptible to slipping towards the concrete reactivity myself. The deanimating pull to the "unchangeable" presents itself in many guises. For example, early in our work Ms C made frequent significant steps forwards in terms of feeling understood and finding that I had food for thought that could help her grow. But almost predictably these "realisations" were followed by a sense of suspicion about our work, a feeling that I was fraudulent, only out to rob her, only wanting her money, that I wanted her to remain stuck so that I could bleed her dry of funds. In these circumstances we have understood that her envious wish to rob me of my resources is what triggers her conviction that I am intent on being a thief of what is valuable to her.

But when I feel caught off-guard by these denigrating distortions, my immediate experience can be a flash of defensive fury, such as "Here after all our work, and your recent gain, you see me as this money-grubbing figure ... you are dragging down our good hard work … and I won't have it." At these times I have had to do a bit of intense inner work in order to gain the wider view that I am being drawn into the concrete retaliatory place; this recognition—plus a few deep breaths—generally help me to regain my analytic stance and to recognise that I have just taken in but not yet metabolised a concrete projection of fraud and greed, rather than being able to maintain my separate-minded awareness of the hard work at hand, while also appreciating the pull from that concrete aspect. As well, I want to remain clear-eyed about what was going on if my patient is to gain any clarity about and thus rescue from this situation. Sometimes it seems that these denigrating encounters are hate- or envy-fuelled, but at other times I have come to feel that the entropic forces towards meaninglessness are not so intentional, but just, as Sandler suggests, that they press relentlessly and impersonally to prevail.

Occasionally I have considered whether my guilt over being away and thus causing pain, perhaps even re-traumatising my patient, might impede my ability to be the fully receiving, containing object whom she needs. I think that the analyst at times can be so overwhelmed by her own guilt in causing such a painful repetition of loss that only in retrospect can she fully see how her guilt prolonged the concrete situation. On more than one occasion with Ms C, who approached my breaks with great apprehension, I found it very difficult to be deeply empathic with the pain my absence was about to bring. Instead I would shift into a defensive position of slight irritation or impatience with Ms C's "over-reacting" to my upcoming absence, or at other times, I might subtly nudge my patient to do something or be positive, or to find the opportunity in the absence. These postures of mine would convey not a guilt-free, patient mind for her pain but a guilt-tinged impatience, which left her feeling bereft if she could not remain "happy" for the duration. On these occasions, only when I returned from being away could I see how abandoned my guilt had made her feel. And the repair at these times involved my careful attention to how dismissed she felt deep down when she experienced me to be urging her to be "happy" rather than to accompany her in the upcoming pain of my absence. My finally being able to offer a patient, receptive, undefensive mind, even after the fact, went quite a ways in terms of providing a container for that pain while also finally accompanying her in that effort. In addition my patient felt affirmed in her experience that I had indeed missed her pain, and I was reminded of how encumbering emotions such as guilt can be to the analyst's clarity and working capacities.

Concluding considerations

In review, concrete experience is intense and vivid; it often resides indelibly in memory as well as in the body, and it carries a punch that seems to declare its intense assertions as unassailable truths. It returns to the fore via the process of concretisation whenever our capacities for reflective thought are strained or depleted, whether from internal or external sources. Indeed, our uncontained emotions, felt as intense sensory onslaught, or clothed as withering doubt, seem able to trigger this concretising function which appears to exert an entropic, deanimating pull upon thought, easily dismantling its products into their sensory elements and thus reconverting the "thinkable" into the more ancient "unthinkable" sensory state. It may be that concrete functioning and thought are two poles of an evolutionary spectrum, with the more ancient and now hard-wired modality inevitably drawing our valiant thinking efforts back to the sensory bedrock that is so ingrained.

Reflective thought presents much more quietly. Within bounded mental space, being open to various possibilities, we can feel tentative in our quest amid uncertainty. In this softer scape, derived from and also giving rise to human reverie, the experience of being held in mind and emotionally known provides potential transformation of the "unthinkable". Even so, the products of thought and reverie as part of our everyday humanity cannot enduringly resist the relentless forces of concretisation. It may be, however, that another possible source of reverie that embraced by the well-attended dream, has the potential to do so.

The remembered dream may be sturdy in appearance or only fleetingly so, but to the interested mind the dream seems to be able to express a deep wisdom. One important element here may be the quality of the receiving mind, such as my providing a mind which could hold on to and think about the dream which my patient would initially only have dismissed. This attentiveness may provide a model of sturdiness regarding value for the dream, that is, space to regard its messages, such as a fire escape past the chaotic childhood family, or the loyalty to the militant explosiveness. Thus the dream messages, received and thought about, might lead to steps towards transcendence of the chaos and "noise" of entrenchment and deanimation.

And yet the wisdom of the dream does not seem to reside in the interplay between the receiving mind and the dream itself. Indeed, it feels like the dream messages "come" from a place beyond what the usual listening mind can provide. The wisdom of the dream may derive from the binocular capacity of the dreaming process, that discourse between conscious and unconscious regions, from which messages may emerge relatively erosion-free to be further protected by the receiving mind. My being able to hold onto the dreams for my patient seemed to allow her then to think about the dreams' messages, but the wisdom of the messages—of loyalty to militant explosiveness, or the fire escape possibilities—these messages, it is suggested, derived from that internal binocular discourse.

The pairing of our attentive minds with the wisdom of the dream may allow investigations beyond our current considerations. Just as the animating capacities of human reverie give added dimension and "knowability" to concrete experience, the animating capacities of binocular dream-reverie partnered with our attentiveness may foster a "getting to know" into deeper regions of the psyche.

Are these contemplations a flight of fantasy? Perhaps, but with the dream as a guide or perhaps as a co-pilot it is intriguing to ponder just where our future psychoanalytic investigations might lead.

References

Anderson, M. (1999). The pressure toward enactment and the hatred of reality. *Journal of the American Psychoanalytic Association, 47*: 503–517.

Bion, W. R. (1962). A theory of thinking. *International Journal of Psychoanalysis, 43*: 306–310.

Damasio, A. (2003). *Looking for Spinoza, Joy, Sorrow and the Feeling Brain.* Orlando, FL: Harcourt.

Grotstein, J. (2009). Dreaming as a "curtain of illusion": revisiting the "royal road" with Bion as our guide. *International Journal of Psychoanalysis, 90*: 733–753.

Meltzer, D. (1968). Terror, persecution and dread: a dissection of paranoid anxieties. *International Journal of Psychoanalysis, 49*: 396–400.

Ogden, T. (2009). *Rediscovering Psychoanalysis, Thinking and Dreaming, Learning and Forgetting.* London: Routledge.

Sandler, P. C. (1997). The apprehension of psychic reality: extensions of Bion's theory of alpha-function. *International Journal of Psychoanalysis, 78*: 43–52.

CHAPTER TWO

Content and process in the treatment of concrete patients

Alan Bass

One of the great difficulties of working with "concrete" patients is having the flexibility to move back and forth between traditional and novel forms of interpretation. To explain what I mean, I have to give a summary of my basic ideas about concreteness.

We are all familiar with the problem: the patient who appears analysable, but resists any interpretation that presumes meaning and symbolisation. Strangely, though, the patient stays in analysis. One of the earliest examples in the literature is from 1919. Karl Abraham writes about patients who can tolerate no interpretations, instead arguing with the analyst about who is "right", and yet showing a "never wearying readiness to be analyzed" (p. 304). Abraham uses all the theory at his disposition at the time to explain this "special form of resistance"—defiance, anality, sadism, narcissism, auto-eroticism, envy. But he cannot conceive of something about the interpretive process itself that would provoke such intense resistance.

Integrating many sources, reflecting upon my own clinical work and that of supervisees, I came to the conclusion that concreteness is a compromise formation that defends against the *possibility* of meaning and symbolisation (Bass, 2000). The possibility of meaning and symbolisation is difference. The assumption that a symptom, a dream, a behaviour, and, most important, the relation to the analyst can be meaningful presumes that something is related, but not identical, to something else; they are different. To interpret that "x" means "y" is a differentiating process. Many analysts have emphasised that the concrete insistence that "x" can only mean "x" is due to separation anxiety. This is half true, because difference implies separation. But difference also implies connection: "x" is not "y" (they are separate), but "x" is related to "y" (they are connected).

To cite two major influences on my thinking: Loewald (1960) thought that every interpretation implies the differential between the patient and the analyst and that the "therapeutic action of psychoanalysis" is the internalisation of this differential; Winnicott (1951) said that symbolisation depends upon paradoxical transitionality, simultaneous separation and connection (difference itself). However, neither Loewald nor Winnicott thought about defences against difference and transitionality. In scattered places, Freud offered some crucial, unintegrated insights on this question. In *Group Psychology* (1921c) he wrote of a primordial, aggressive-defensive response to difference, and in *Beyond the Pleasure Principle* (1920 g) he understood Eros, the simultaneously self preservative and libidinal life-drive, as a tension raising separating-integrating force of difference. True to his conviction that the pleasure principle always aims at tension reduction, Freud called Eros a tension raising "mischief maker" (1923b, p. 46). The death drive, the counter-force of Eros, is then the tension reducing force of dedifferentiation.

Some contemporary Kleinians have made important contributions on this topic. Betty Joseph, in an early paper on the repetition compulsion and the death drive, wrote of patients who drain all interpretations of meaning in order to resist the analyst's embodiment of Eros, the life drive; these patients, she considers, suffer more from contact than from loss (1959). In a related vein, John Steiner uses the concept of psychic retreats to understand patients who avoid meaningful contact with the analyst (1993). My view is that defences against differentiated contact are an unconscious retreat from Eros's tension raising, paradoxical (transitional) aspects. Such defences against Eros interfere with its function as libidinal self-preservation. This is why concrete patients almost always manifest difficulties with both self care and connection to themselves and others. To put it formulaically: Eros's self-preservative function is split from its libidinal function, enhancing the tendency towards tension reduction (the death drive). This is an affective and cognitive process: the patient is warding off the tension of differentiation, and so often cannot reflect upon anything the analyst says that might be helpful. Hence, the patient defends against the *process* that makes meaning possible, not against specific content.

Two major clinical problems emerge. How does one address defence against the process that makes meaning possible? And when does one use traditional forms of intervention which presume meaning? Concrete patients sometimes speak in a way that allows the analyst to interpret in a content oriented way. The analyst usually breathes a sigh of relief: analytic work as he/she understands it can finally take place. But the patient never stays in this position; typically the analyst then despairs of the effectiveness of the treatment. And what about those moments when a patient who usually responds to traditional forms of interpretation becomes surprisingly concrete? Are such moments swept under the rug? The primordial defensive response to difference/Eros implies that we are all internally divided between tension raising life and tension reducing death, between differentiation and dedifferentiation. Anyone can be concrete at times.

Because concreteness does interfere with cognition, it is often viewed as a deficit. As a defensive response to the possibility of meaning, however, I view it as a compromise formation. As in any compromise formation, what is defended against is unconsciously "there". If the patient is defending against tension raising, paradoxical difference, this difference must have been registered. How to understand this phenomenon? This is where I draw upon Freud's conception of disavowal (1927e). Disavowal is a way of describing ego splitting: one simultaneously does and does not know something. One oscillates between the knowing and the not knowing. Freud describes this process as the registration and repudiation of reality, a process exemplified by fetishism. However, I believe that Freud was inconsistent in his description of fetishism. He described it as a disavowal of the "reality of castration", a clear oxymoron. In my view, fetishism is a disavowal of the reality of sexual difference, and is more complex than Freud thought. As a defence against sexual difference, fetishism first registers this reality and then repudiates it, creating a primary oscillation. The fetishistic compromise formation replaces sexual difference with the fantasy that it equals phallic or castrated. There is then a secondary oscillation between phallic and castrated, as described by Freud (Bass, 2000).

Concrete compromise formations do the same thing. There is a primary registration and repudiation of difference. The real difference repudiated is then replaced by two opposed fantasies conflated with reality. This substitution produces a black or white, all or nothing, objectively right or objectively wrong conception of reality, which replaces those aspects of reality which cannot fit into these categories; difference itself is a "both and" not an "either or" reality. But just as the fetishist has to have been made anxious by registered sexual difference, so concrete defences indicate an anxious response to a registered differentiating process, manifesting itself as resistance to interpretation *per se* in treatment. Always keeping in mind that concreteness is also a defence against tension raising, libidinal self-preservative Eros, one can begin to understand why concrete patients are threatened by the possibility of interpretive help.

The anxieties aroused by differentiation are closer to the traumatic end of the spectrum. When one repudiates the "reality of difference" via a system of opposed fantasies, to re-experience what has been repudiated feels uncontrollably chaotic. The concrete patient talks to the analyst, "free associates", in order to prevent the re-emergence of such intense anxiety. In other words, despite coming to treatment and apparent compliance with the fundamental rule, the patient is speaking in order to prevent an analytic process from taking place. The possibility of interpretation becomes the threat of loss of control over reality. The analyst must intervene carefully in a defensive process which will lead to re-experiencing near-traumatic levels of anxiety. The concrete patient can be on the verge of panic if he or she actually experiences interpretive help. It is counterintuitive, but necessary, to understand that what the patient is paying us for is precisely what threatens him or her the most.

To show how all this emerges clinically, I will give an example from two sessions of a supervised case. Mr A, in his mid-thirties, is a professional actor. An only child, Mr A's "liberal" parents exposed him to adult sexuality in early childhood. His father died during his adolescence. He began treatment towards the end of his professional training. He was near graduation from a fine conservatory, but was doing everything he could to sabotage it. He did not hand in necessary forms, was obstreperous with teachers and administrators, and lived in chaos. He had difficulties following through on anything that involved self care. For example, he had an opportunity to work abroad, but waited until the very last minute to try to find his passport. He could not find it, and so had to forego the opportunity. He had great difficulties relating to people, tending to spend a great deal of time sleeping, online, or compulsively practising acting parts in a way that did nothing to improve his skills. And he had a sexual fetish of which he was deeply ashamed: his sexual interest in women was confined to their feet.

Dr B was midway in her training when Mr A was referred to her. She had two very difficult problems to deal with from the start. As one might expect, Mr A wanted a woman analyst precisely because he would be aroused by her shoes and feet. And he was as obstreperous with Dr B as he was with all authority figures, to the point of throwing pillows off the couch when he was angry. One could reasonably wonder about a borderline personality organisation, but the course of Mr A's treatment did not bear out this diagnosis. Eventually his obstreperous behaviour faded away. He did not graduate from the conservatory, because he was offered a job in a professional company, which he accepted. At the time of the sessions to be reported, Mr A had lost and regained this job. He was chronically plagued by insecurities about his masculinity because of his foot fetishism, and was still prone to not taking care of the necessities of everyday life.

Mr A was markedly concrete in treatment. He often responded to interpretations by accusing Dr B of criticising him. In a way he was right. Dr B had all the typical countertransference responses to a concrete patient: she often felt frustrated, overwhelmed, confused, unable to think, and incredulous—"You can't possibly be for real when you say that." But she persisted and Mr A persisted. There were often difficulties about payment, but Mr A always eventually paid what he owed. Over time Dr B was able to raise his fee. At the time of the sessions Mr A had just ended a relationship, his first.

Mr A begins the session by talking about a hiking trip he had taken with friends earlier in the day. He goes on to say: "I sort of feel like I don't know what to talk about right now. I am trying to remember what we talked about at the end of the last session. Vaguely I remember talking about the idea of my difficulty staying in reality, and how it was connected to my fear of establishing relationships with people. I guess I was making a point about that, but I don't remember what it was that led me to talk about that." He yawns. "Excuse me."

There is nothing unusual about a patient having difficulty remembering something that had felt important in the previous session.

The analyst naturally thinks of the need to re-establish defences. But note the topic: staying in reality, establishing relationships, i.e., connectedness. From long experience, Dr B also knows that Mr A retreats from these issues by sleeping, and he yawns here. I take the yawn to be an expression of Mr A's unconscious need to protect himself from the tension of connecting to reality and other people, and also to himself, to what he was saying in the previous session. Dr B and I have often discussed this topic, and she intervenes along those lines here, saying "So this is also about not being with yourself." Her words are simple, but they convey a complex thought: Mr B uses splitting and disavowal not only in relation to reality and other people, but also in relation to his own inner processes.

Dr B's intervention here illustrates some important aspects of interpretation of defence against differentiating process. She is addressing Mr A's affective-cognitive experience as he speaks, his state of "being": "This is also about not being with yourself." She does not address specific content, nor does she say anything about why Mr A has difficulty being with himself. This last point is critical. Our usual assumption is that when we address meaning, we also address causality: you say or do "x", *because* it means "y". But when we address defence against the possibility of meaning, we have to free ourselves of any suggestion of causality, which always implies the differential relation between "x" and "y".

Analysts are trained to think in terms of meaning and causality. Hence, it is very difficult for us to refrain from making causal interpretations. When patients resist interpretation itself we tend to revert to some form of suggesting that we know what things mean and why they happen. We think that we know all this because we are analysts. However, clinical experience with concrete patients consistently shows that the implication of meaning and causality leads to power struggles over who is "right". (This is what happened between Abraham and his patient.) I have found this to be an almost generic countertransference response to concrete patients, which often leads to concreteness in the analyst. Dr B and I had spent a long time in supervision discussing this issue. When the analyst feels devalued and frustrated because the patient dismisses his or her knowledge, the analyst is tempted to depart from neutrality. Because it is so difficult to sustain the attack on one's knowledge and competence, the analyst may either try to reassert some kind of authority, or retreat into defensive silence. Unfortunately, the departure from neutrality plays right into the patient's need to engage in a defensive power struggle, in which there is always a winner and a loser. That is why it is important that Dr B is effectively neutral in her simple intervention about Mr A's not wanting to be with himself. She has not retreated, and is not speaking from the position of confusion, despair, frustration, and the need to prove she is right.

Mr A says: "Yeah, those things are somewhat connected"—an unusual response for him. He pauses, and goes on to speak about the woman he has been involved with, Ms C. "I'm thinking about how difficult it was for me to be with C … A lot of the difficulty had to do with us not being compatible, but overall I didn't know how to be with her. I was always fighting to create space, instead of allowing myself to be with her. The tension of being with her was too much for me to handle."

Mr A had also spoken a great deal about wanting to fondle and lick Ms C's feet. He had been too ashamed to ask her. Much of his sexual history did seem to explain *why* he was a foot fetishist. He vividly remembered feelings of revulsion, stimulation, and inadequacy related to seeing his mother's naked body.

Mr A then says: "I think the reason I did that was because the tension of being with her was too much for me to handle." Here, I want to speak of my own response as supervisor. Dr B and I had a long-standing, good relationship. She was very eager to learn. At times, however, she coped with the difficulties of treating Mr A by using what I said in a didactic way, as if she could resolve his difficulties by teaching him what she was learning from me. We also talked about this issue in the supervision. When Mr A speaks of the tension of being with Ms C, I wonder if he is parroting Dr B. I was concerned about compliance and intellectualisation, even parallel process: I was teaching Dr B and she was teaching Mr A. I did not intervene, however, waiting to hear what happened next. Referring to Mr A's statement about a tension that was too much to handle, Dr B asked: "What kind of tension did you experience?" Mr A said: "I guess being with her represented a sense of being in reality. It was so much and so difficult that I was trying to escape from it, but that way of managing tension added another level of tension and anxiety, and I was trying to fight against that too." As I listen I am divided in my thoughts: Mr A does sound possibly compliant and intellectualised, but he is also possibly connecting to himself in a non-defensive way. And he is describing the kind of galloping anxiety I expect to hear when concrete patients begin to experience "differentiated connection", whether in analysis or in life. So I still wait. Dr B reports that Mr A paused and then said: "I feel like I'm having trouble connecting with you today. I'm having thoughts about my way of being with you. I can't understand the reason. I am feeling afraid."

This is an even more unusual comment from Mr A. He reflects upon his internal experience of Dr B, rather than concretely objecting to her "criticism" of him, or parroting by rote what he has learned. My thought at this point is that Dr B's simple interventions, which have described Mr A's experiences without attributing meaning or causality to them, have been effective. He is not intellectualised or compliant. But my hypothesis is that entering into this analytic space will make Mr A even more anxious, leading him to retreat to concreteness.

Dr B asks him what he is afraid of. He says: "I wonder if I'm afraid of talking about the thoughts I have about my relationship to you." Dr B says "Uh-huh." Mr A pauses and continues: "I think one of the things that happens is—when I talk to you, I feel the need to go over what I did during the day and think about whether or not I have been good or bad. I didn't really think about doing that today because I went hiking, so that automatically meant I was doing good. So it meant that I didn't have to be concerned about doing good today. But I'm wondering—feeling relaxed about that makes me feel like I am doing something wrong. Every time I talk to you, I go through this process. Talking to you feels like a confession to me … Is it a good thing that I approach talking to you in this way? I'm wondering what you think … I guess I was wondering what you think of me … One of the things that happens is—when I talk to you, I am coming from the point of view of being alone. I find it easier to talk to you if I approach you from that place of being alone rather than speaking from a shared space with you. I find it difficult to do that, so every time I talk to you, I am fighting not to be in that shared space."

These associations bear detailed commentary. As I listened, my sense was that Mr A was approaching the anxiety about actually being in an analytic process. When the patient internalises the transitional space between himself and the analyst, so that there is also transitional space within himself, opening the possibility of meaning and symbolisation, he panics. Mr A accurately describes how he generally copes with the possibility of this kind of anxiety. He concretely and fetishistically divides his experiences into good and bad, and anticipates what will happen if he tells the analyst about his good or bad experiences.

While this sounds like typical superego projection, Mr A has concretely insisted that this is *really* how Dr B listens to him. Because he went hiking with friends—i.e., did not spend the day retreating into his fantasy world—Mr A says he has done "good". But what if his confidence about having done "good" is false, what if he is "too relaxed", is caught off guard, and then is made to feel he has been "bad"? In other words, he concretely experiences the analyst as a "superego fetish". He girds himself for his sessions by swinging back and forth between these two fantasies conflated with reality. But then he explains that he does this so that he can remain convinced that when he speaks to Dr B he is not in a shared space, is not connected to her. Although he is literally in the room with her, psychically he is alone, as he says. In fact, he has to destroy shared psychic space, which he does via his concrete, "superego fetish" fantasy construction. In terms of process, this is the manifestation of tension raising, connecting-separating, differentiating life, versus tension reducing, dedifferentiating, destructive death. These two forces are always intertwined in the concrete transference. When Mr A registers the reality of differentiating space, he has to repudiate it.

Dr B asks Mr A how he fights against being in a shared space with her. He responds: "By wishing that the session is over, or by wondering about what you are thinking about me." Mr A makes clear that he wants to use wish fulfilment to get out of the shared time and space of the session, and that he uses his image of Dr B as a "superego fetish" in the same way. He then goes on to say: "Before I came here today I was dozing off. I'm still feeling sleepy." As in his yawning earlier in the session, for Mr A sleep is the ultimate retreat from the tension raising, time-space of analysis. But he continues to speak about it—progress for him. He says: "I'm trying to tell you that it is not easy for me to know how to really connect with you and stay connected with you … I am pushing against that connection—I am trying to push it away from me … My thought is that I have been good, so I don't want or need to talk to you. I want to come back and talk to you when I feel as though I am not being good." In other words, unless he is concretely "bad", and so deserving of criticism from Dr B, Mr A would rather not be there. This raises another important point. While Mr A has complained about Dr B's "criticism" of him, we see here that the "criticism" is preferable to sustaining an interpretive process. He needs to feel the protection of his concrete good-bad fantasies.

Here Dr B says: "You wish to make me into a parental figure." I am uncomfortable with this intervention. Just as it is difficult for the concrete patient to stay with the anxiety about engagement in the analytic process, so it is difficult for the analyst to stay there with the patient. The analyst can relieve his or her own tension by returning to content oriented, causal interpretations. Is Dr B doing that here? One does not know for sure: her intervention can go either way. Dr B goes on to say: "If you don't turn me into a parental figure, you will be more frightened about the kind of connection you have with me in a shared time and space." My internal reaction is like the one I mentioned above: I wonder whether Dr B is using what we have discussed in supervision to make sure she is doing the right thing. Is she being good for me?

Mr A responds: "That's true—but I can't pinpoint where the source of that anxiety is." Mr A is saying something that our theories of anxiety do not usually tell us. We are accustomed to thinking about signal anxiety, separation anxiety, traumatic anxiety, persecutory anxiety, depressive anxiety (to use the major Freudian, ego psychological, and Kleinian categories), but not the kind of all-pervasive anxiety Mr A speaks about. One might think about "free floating anxiety", neurotic anxiety with an unknown source. However, Mr A is saying that he knows his anxiety is about his connection to Dr B, but that he doesn't know where it is coming from. There is an apparently non-psychoanalytic way of thinking about this kind of anxiety. Heidegger (1996) conceives of existential anxiety, *Angst*, as an all-pervasive, non-localisable feeling about what we *are*, about our existence as creatures who are always in a world that we are open to. This kind of openness is also for Heidegger the time and space of interpretation. I find this a useful way to think about what Mr A says here. As he stays connected to his fear of being in a shared time and space with Dr B, a time and space in which he is open to the process, he also experiences something enigmatic: he cannot "pinpoint" where this anxiety comes from. Heidegger says that *Angst* comes from everywhere and nowhere. For patients who defend against differentiation, being in the open time and space of an interpretive process is too strange, too overwhelming, too nearly traumatic.

After saying that he cannot pinpoint the source of his anxiety, Mr A says: "If I am able to exist in the shared time and space and connect with you, it will make me realise that escaping to fantasy is not adequate. I push against that thought because I am afraid of realising that I need other people. I am holding on to the fantasy that being alone is good, because being in reality is scary for me." This is a cogent statement of the concrete patient's dilemma. To conflate one's fantasies with reality is in the everyday sense to be alone, and in the more technical sense to exist in an auto-erotic, wish fulfilling world in which the need for anything other than oneself is eliminated. To feel the need for others, to be open to something other than oneself, to be in reality, is, again, to re-experience an all-pervasive anxiety. Dr B asks, "What's so scary about it [i.e., needing other people, being in reality]?" Mr A answers, "Not being able to be with people and people not being there for me. I'm afraid of finding out that I'm not able to find anyone to be with."

Here I think that Mr A is understandably getting away from the intensity of his anxiety. My thought is that he is most afraid of finding that someone *is* there for him, especially his analyst. My hope is that Dr B will say something about this to Mr A, but that can also be concreteness in the supervisor, not allowing for the supervisee's different thoughts. In fact, Dr B does say something unlike what I am thinking. She intervenes: "I wonder if what you are saying is that you are afraid that your approach to yourself will not change, so that at the end of this long process, you will not get what you deserve." I am a bit jarred by this interpretation, thinking that it is too far from what Mr A is saying. Mr A responds: "I think you are saying something very different from what I am saying." In my opinion, Mr A is right; Dr B has made a leap here. But in terms of clinical process, this is another unusual moment. Mr A is able to *think* about Dr B's intervention, able to consider that it is *different* from what he has said without feeling criticised, without engaging in a power struggle, without retreating into concreteness. Could it be that enough work on defence against process, motivated by all-pervasive anxiety, has been done to allow Mr A to tolerate the differentiating process of interpretation for a while?

Dr B explains her last intervention: "What I am saying is—your way of avoiding building a connection is a direct reflection of how you treat yourself." Mr A: "When I heard you say that I somehow started feeling like I was undeserving of being in the world and being happy." It seems that Mr A is confirming Dr B's interpretation about not getting what he deserves. Here, then, I have to change gear. Perhaps Dr B's analytic intuition was correct, and it was time to begin working on content. Dr B continues in a content oriented vein: "What did you do that was so bad that you do not deserve to be happy?" Mr A: "When you asked me that, the feeling of guilt about living came up. It's associated with how I am living and my dad is dead. That speaks to my fear and all the trouble I've had connecting with people. I didn't feel sad when he passed, so I felt I was not a good person. I felt like I was a psychopath, a sociopath. Another thing that comes to mind is—I think, maybe, in order to have a real connection with people I have to be able to look at myself and feel okay about what I see in myself. I find it hard to look at myself and think about my sexual desire, and at the same time, not to feel ashamed of it."

We are now on familiar analytic ground. Mr A had been conflicted about his father's long illness and deterioration during his adolescence, and over-stimulated and intimidated by both parents' "liberal" sexual attitudes when he was young. His foot fetishism is a complex compromise deriving from issues of sexuality, death, castration, anality, masochism, and defence against sexual difference. It is the intersection of content and process issues. Immediately after speaking about his shame, Mr A says: "I don't know. I am talking about my sexual desire, but I wonder if this is a way of seeking to escape from you." Again, he is unusually self-reflective, and able to think about the transference. Dr B responds: "It is almost as though you are saying that exploring what is going on with you and connecting with me can't happen simultaneously. These two things are somehow contradictory to one another." My sense is that Mr A and Dr B are now working together productively. Mr A can see how he might use content as a defence against process; Dr B addresses his difficulty integrating content and process—which itself is a process oriented intervention, without direct causal implication.

Mr A responds: "I think that's true ... Being with you forces me to be with me, and I find that extremely uncomfortable ... I do everything I can to prevent myself from facing who I am ... I am thinking that I can't be with other people unless I am being with myself. I notice there is a sense of self-hatred or shame associated with that idea. I can't accept that I am unable to connect with people—I feel like I am always running away from that awareness. I am afraid of putting myself in reality and connecting with people. I guess I am talking about the tension of being with myself and applying that to being with people ... I wonder if there is something about this sense of who I am that makes it harder for me to stay in reality, take care of myself, and really try connecting with people ... I am wondering what you are thinking." Dr B: "I am thinking that all of these things you are telling me apply to the work we doing together." Mr A responds by describing the fetishistic compromise formation which registers and repudiates engagement in the process: "My mind is going to this place where it is telling me things are this way or that way. I am attempting to escape from this moment by setting up a kind of dichotomy, two oppositional views."

Dr B again intervenes very simply: "Does that mean you are feeling uncomfortable right now?" Mr A assents, and Dr B asks him if he has any idea why. He says: "Because I am feeling confused. It feels as though things are undetermined right now." In other words, Mr A knows at this moment that he would prefer to escape by retreating to his fetish-istic dichotomies which give him a feeling of control over reality, but he stays in the moment. Doing so takes him to a place of confusion and indetermination. His anxiety is escalating. He says: "Maybe I don't understand what you mean …" Mr A's "maybe" indicates that he is vacillating between understanding and not understanding, meaning and non-meaning. He had understood Dr B a moment ago, but since staying with understanding takes him to a place of confusion and inde-termination; he wants to retreat. He starts to go back to his concrete conviction that Dr B is criticising him: "Maybe you were pointing out that I was not relating to you." But then he comes back: "Maybe by say-ing what I just said, when I am relating to you, I feel like I am conduct-ing a form of retreat … I find it difficult to both look into myself and understand how I am being with you … I don't know how to do that without feeling the need to escape from the moment when I am with you." Mr A's direct statement of his conflict over exactly what analysis is—looking into oneself and understanding how one is relating to the analyst—helps him to emerge from the concrete conviction that Dr B is criticising him: "Your comment did not mean to say that I was miss-ing the point …." But this emergence from concreteness again increases his anxiety: "This entire conversation is making me feel really anxious. It feels very undetermined. I feel like the anxiety I am experiencing is not helpful. Maybe I have trouble experiencing that kind of anxiety—at this point our conversation is making me feel like it is not healthy for me to experience this much anxiety. I feel like there is no point in expe-riencing anxiety in this way." The session ends.

There is no way to know for sure at the end of the session whether Mr A has been helped or not by experiencing this much anxiety. He claims he has not been helped, but my sense is that he probably has been. To shake his concrete certainties, to modify his defences against engagement in the process, is to deal with his most important transference-resistance. This is the crux of every analysis, and is always difficult. It is particularly difficult for the concrete patient for just the reason Mr A describes: it takes him to the paradoxical place where effective interpretive help produces near-traumatic anxiety. One hopes that even though Mr A ended the session by saying that there was "no point" in sustaining such a difficult experience, he will unconsciously put it to work. But there is always the risk that he will retreat further into his self encapsulated auto-erotic world, as he has done so many times in the past.

Generalised defence against analytic process is often directed against all the factors that make interpretation possible, including the analytic frame itself. We have seen Mr A's reactions to sustaining shared space; retrospectively it is possible to wonder whether his throwing of pillows at the beginning of his treatment was a concrete expression of an imperative need to attack that space. The analytic frame is also temporal, and difference itself has a temporal aspect: as simultaneous separation and connection it is not immediately present, but is an expression of what is "not now". Another aspect of concrete compromise formations, with their urgent immediacy, is their insistence on the "now". Difference is a tension to be eliminated *now*. Things are what they are *now*. One has to know who is right or wrong, in control or out of control *now*. Now is the time of wish fulfilment. Dreams, Freud says, have only one temporal mode—the present (1900a, p. 566). Lateness or non-attendance become ways of controlling time. Mr A neither missed nor was late for the next session, typical occurrences for him in the past. The simple fact that Mr A arrives for the next session on time may indicate that he was helped in the previous session.

I will not give as much detail about this session, but will emphasise how the question of confining time to the *now* in order to control the process eventually emerged. Mr A begins by recounting a long talk he had the previous night with Ms C. He says that he really never cared as much about her as she did about him, and that he doesn't miss her that much. But he wonders whether he is avoiding any feeling of loss. He says: "I guess I sense there is a strong connection to her, and I want to push that away—I want to get myself away from that ... I pull myself away from the emotional connection I have with her. I am hoping that I will change my ways by talking to you ... I want this to be over so I can be all by myself again ... I want to keep thinking I have the option to escape. I don't like that part of me because more and more I feel like the act of escaping takes me to a dangerous place. But in the moment when I am seeking to escape, that is what I want to do and I expect that doing so will make me feel better." Mr A lucidly articulates his dilemma: connection to anyone—Ms C, Dr B, and himself—is too much for him. He wants to convince himself that escape is justifiable.

As the session proceeds, my sense is that Dr B herself is having trouble with Mr A's justifications for escape. She again becomes didactic, telling Mr A that when he retreats he is in fantasy, asking him if he is willing to spend the rest of his life in fantasy. He says that he is not getting any benefit from talking to her. He also says that he doesn't take care of everyday issues, because doing so will make him feel lonely. One can empathise with Dr B here: Mr A uses contradictory arguments—he wants to be alone, he is afraid of being alone—to support his arguments for escape. My thought is that although Mr A's on time arrival at the session indicates an increased tolerance of his anxiety about the analytic process, he is now using the session to avoid this anxiety. And in fact he says: "I am afraid that therapy will make me feel anxious—it will make me deal with anxiety that I am trying not to experience in my whole life."

We know how easy it is for the supervisor to assume a superior position. The difficult balance is to be realistic that one should know more than the supervisee, but that it is all too easy to know what to do when one is not on the "firing line" of the session. My sense is that Dr B should remain silent after Mr A's last statement, to let his words reverberate, and to see where he goes. But the pressure from Mr A was apparently too much. Dr B explains to him that experiencing anxiety and talking about it are helpful to him. I think that this is a non-neutral intervention. Mr A was clear about his resistance to the analytic process, a statement to be honoured. As Dr B tries to convince Mr A of the value of the analysis, he becomes more focused on time. He says: "I would like to know from you—how can I use therapy in a helpful way even in the next ten minutes?" It is as if Mr A is saying to Dr B: since you are telling me that the therapy is helpful, prove it, make it helpful *now*. Make it helpful in the ten minutes I still have to endure. He is using the actual clock time of the session to put Dr B in an even more impossible position than when he said he both wanted to be alone and was afraid of being alone. He is becoming concrete, but in part, I think, as a response to Dr B's non-neutral interventions, which abet his defences.

However, Mr A does not entirely lose his understanding of himself: "I am feeling so anxious right now, and I don't know what the source of this anxiety is. Am I feeling anxious because I am recognising I am wasting my time right now? ... In a few minutes I will stop talking to you, but I am wishing this moment to happen sooner, so I don't have to continue talking to you right now ... I don't know what I want from therapy. I want it to be over so I don't have to think about what we have talked about." Mr A is on the cusp of meaning and non-meaning, of registering the analytic process and repudiating it.

Dr B says: "Well, ironically the point of therapy is for you to continue thinking about what we talked about while we were connecting with each other." What is the status of this intervention? Is Dr B still in the didactic, non-neutral place, or, by stating what is apparently most self-evident about the analytic process, has she addressed Mr A's most important transference-resistance? He responds: "That seems like a simple idea, but I have not done that for a long time. But hearing you mention that is helpful. What I often do, instead, is to push away what we talked about because the anxiety is so much ... I feel relieved that the session is over. I then feel like I could finally go on the internet, or do something that would make the anxiety go away ... If I have to hold on to the anxiety I don't know what I will do with it. I look at the clock just now because my anxiety is so strong. I want to go back into fantasy ... I know I need to talk to you about my anxiety, but I know that the time is almost over." Dr B: "How do you feel about the fact that we have to end the session at this moment?" Mr A: "I feel fine about it."

One sees in these two sessions an oscillation between toleration of anxiety and retreat from it, between registration of the possibility of an analytic process and repudiation of it, between sustaining the open time-space of differentiating connection and retreat to the closed auto-erotic now. This oscillation also characterises the overall arc of these analyses; the analyst can never stop moving back and forth between process and content interpretations. One cannot underestimate how difficult this is for the analyst. Recently, after moving ahead professionally, Mr A regressed to the kind of action he had demonstrated at the beginning of his treatment: he kicked open a door to make a rehearsal possible. However, he immediately understood what he had done, and took steps to remedy the situation. In the next session, he paid Dr B for two months of treatment, an internalisation of the frame. He said: "When I pay you, I feel open to you. I want to avoid that."

I want to express my profound gratitude to Dr B for providing me with this process material, and for her devotion to Mr A's treatment.

References

Abraham, K. (1919). A special form of resistance to the psychoanalytic method. In *Selected Papers on Psychoanalysis*. London: Maresfield Reprints, 1927.

Bass, A. (2000). *Difference and Disavowal: The Trauma of Eros*. Palo Alto, CA: Stanford University Press.

Freud, S. (1900a). *The Interpretation of Dreams. S. E., 4–5*. London: Hogarth.

Freud, S. (1920g). *Beyond the Pleasure Principle. S. E., 18*. London: Hogarth.

Freud, S. (1921c). *Group Psychology and the Analysis of the Ego. S. E., 18*. London: Hogarth.

Freud, S. (1923b). *The Ego and the Id. S. E., 19*. London: Hogarth.

Freud, S. (1927e). Fetishism. *S. E., 21*. London: Hogarth.

Heidegger, M. (1996). *Being and Time*. J. Stambaugh (Trans.). Albany, NY: SUNY Press.

Joseph, B. (1959). An aspect of the repetition compulsion. In: *Psychic Equilibrium and Psychic Change*. London: Routledge, 1989.

Loewald, H. (1960). The therapeutic action of psychoanalysis. In: *Papers on Psychoanalysis*. New Haven, CT: Yale University Press, 1980.

Steiner, J. (1993). *Psychic Retreats*. London: Routledge.

Winnicott, D. W. (1951). Transitional objects and transitional phenomena. In: *From Pediatrics to Psychoanalysis*. New York: Basic Books, 1975.

CHAPTER THREE

Transitional organising experience in analytic process: movements towards symbolising space via the dyad

Joseph A. Cancelmo

Introduction

Psychoanalytic process offers unparalleled opportunities among therapeutic interventions for the transformation of states of concreteness and compromised symbolic capacities that often arise as impasse or stalemates as lived in the transference-countertransference. How these states are conceptualised, and, in turn, navigated by the analytic pair, is seen as central to and facilitative of such potential transformation towards the development of greater symbolic capacity. This chapter attempts to address this potential from both structural and intersubjective perspectives, rather than simply one or the other.

Based on Winnicott's (1951) construct of the transitional realm[1] and rooted in Freudian notions of structuralisation and internalisation (1923b), the shorthand *transitional organising experience* has been suggested to help describe such moments of potential transformation that may arise in an analytic process (Cancelmo, 2009). These moments are viewed as representing compromised internalisations or pathological organisations, based on early empathic failures, impingements, and traumatic experiences, in particular, as they may emerge via the dyad in the analytic process with some of our more challenging patients.

It is the view offered here that such moments represent opportunities for developmental movements of compromised structural and inter-subjective capacities that are the hallmark of the transitional realm and the emergence of symbolisation that it represents.

Both structural and intersubjective frameworks are enshrined in Winnicott's prescient construct of the transitional realm—i.e., the developmental progression from a nascent to a separate self, the organisation of drive experience via the (m)other, and the sorting out of one's own mind in terms of subjectivity and objectivity. These are core products and processes that are forged in early life. While they remain with us as lifelong tensions (Kohut, 1971; Loewald, 1978), what Winnicott (1951) called the "strain of relating inner (subjective) and outer (objective) reality" (p. 240), they are also the basis for creative and authentic exist-ence, a capacity for transitionality[2] in human experience. Ellman (2010) most recently notes that Winnicott likely implied in these words "a con-tinuous dynamic relationship between subject and object (or subject and subject) throughout life" (p. 370), and by extension, in the analytic process.

In the view presented here, less than optimal or pathological devel-opment in these core structural and intersubjective components of the transitional realm inevitably will serve to organise the analytic process and shape the transference-countertransference experience for some of our more concrete patients. This is due, in general, to the illusory qual-ity of analytic experience (Freud, 1914g; Sanville, 1991; Steingart, 1998), and, more specifically, to the inherent ambiguity of the analytic proc-ess in which self and object, active and passive, and past and present are perpetually negotiated (Adler, 1989). "Pathological", as used here, refers to less than optimal outcomes during the transitional phase that are manifest in compromised development in the internalisation of holding-soothing functions, organisation of drive experience, and the development of symbolic capacities, and managed via a range of substi-tutive or prosthetic transitional phenomena (e.g., addictions, psychopa-thy, perversions, and false-self/narcissistic organisations) as described by Winnicott (1951) and extended by others (see Cancelmo, 2009).

Steiner (1993), and more recently Brandchaft (2007), have described pathological organisations of internal object representations based in early traumatic impingements; these internal structures are relatively fixed patterns of reaction and defence that have an addictive, adhesive quality (see also van der Kolk, 1989) and become activated in analytic space as transitional areas. Bollas (1987) likewise described such early compromised experiences in "being and relating" (p. 3), rooted in failures in the earliest caretaking environment, as a "process" experience that inevitably re-emerges via the transference. In the process of analytic regression, the analyst comes to serve as a potentially (new) "transformational object" (Bollas, 1979) providing the background for authentic existence, however compromised, and in that sense, offering potential for transformation via analytic process. Earlier, Bach (1984) described the unfolding of such difficulties and potentialities in the clinical setting as "problems in transitionality", notable in patients' struggles around the boundaries of perception and conceptualisation, subjectivity and objectivity, and more concretely, negotiating transitional areas and moments within the analytic space. From the perspective presented here, the need for the analyst's empathic attunement to the emergence of such moments of potential transformation seems central to the task of articulating the compromised internal structure as lived in the intersubjective space of the transference-countertransference.

Transitional organising experience is seen from this perspective as both organising and also marking movements towards greater symbolic capacities as lived between and within the dyad. In a sense the shorthand *transitional organising experience* might be considered a heuristic tool, a way of thinking about the repetition compulsion in the clinical moment for these patients from both structural and intersubjective perspectives, as embodied by Winnicott's prescient construct of the transitional realm.

This chapter will focus on the ways in which the developmental progression towards greater symbolic capacity is embedded in Winnicott's theory, in conjunction with Contemporary Freudian notions of structuralisation and internalisation, and as elaborated in various ways by others. Particular attention will be paid to his conceptualisation of the earliest experiences with the *environment* and *object* mother and the gradual integration and internalisation of these maternal presences as symbolised in transitional phenomena; these are viewed here as core transference-countertransference configurations that may emerge via the dyad as transitional organising experience (albeit as less than optimal, or compromised attempts to fashion transitionality). Analytic vignettes will serve to illustrate how transitional organising experience may emerge over time: 1) as a repetition of early compromised internal structure and related intersubjective experiences and fantasies rooted in the faulty development of transitionality, 2) as an empathic function of the analyst in the transference-countertransference, and 3) as an articulation of these experiences in ways that foster shifts in symbolising capacities via the dyad. Familiar dynamic constellations[3] that emerge in analytic process over time are also viewed from this perspective as representing opportunities for a re-experiencing (as a two person psychology) and a reorganising (as a one person psychology) towards less "pathological" transitional modes of functioning, allowing for a developmental resumption of transitional (symbolising) space. These vignettes were described in a previous publication (Cancelmo, 2009) and are presented here to describe such nascent shifts in and a resumption of the development of symbolising space via the dyad.

The transitional realm and the development of symbolic capacity

For Winnicott, the transitional realm is a developmental achievement. It is rooted in the bedrock experience with and internalisation of a "good-enough" mother (1960a) as represented in the emergence of symbolic capacities via transitional phenomena. The emergence of transitional phenomena[4] in this sense may be seen as both product and process, a way station in the development of symbolic capacities and the structuralisation they represent.

Winnicott described the infant's experience of mother as taking two forms: 1) the *environment* mother of "quiet" states whose ego protects the infant from impingement and organises early experiences, and 2) the *object* mother of "excited" states experienced as the object of instinctual tensions (Winnicott, 1963a). It is the inevitable (and ideally, optimally timed) misalignments that occur between mother and infant around the provision of these developmental needs that serve to articulate the separateness, and later the subjectivity, objectivity, and interdependence of mother and infant in the intermediate area (Ogden, 1990).

The transitional object represents a pivotal step towards the growing experience of separate, objectively perceived external objects. At this point, mother (as other) is also a subjectively perceived object, still connected to an earlier phase when internal and external, self and other are less differentiated. The paradox and power of the transitional object (and related transitional phenomena) is the capacity to both represent mother and mother's care and to hold as well as to concretely embody mother. Here we have Winnicott's description of the roots of symbolisation (or the aspect of symbolisation that evolves within the object relational sphere). Something stands for something else, i.e., the external object stands for the internal mother and her supplies.

Winnicott (1963b) noted that the needs met by the environment mother and the instinctual wishes associated with the object mother were most likely non-linear and concurrent developmental processes whose coming together is noted in the transitional realm. Bollas (1993) has described these two experiences of mother more broadly as varieties of maternal presence, not so neatly dichotomous, that overlap and inform each other. Abram (1997) underscored the sense of active internal struggling towards an integration of these two mothers in enactments via the transitional object (p. 316) which include, according to Winnicott (1954), "instinctual loving, and also hating, and, if it is a feature, pure aggression" (p. 233).

Winnicott also addressed the ways in which these normal (ideal) developmental processes can go awry due to traumatic experiences (impingements) in the early environment. He noted that resulting failures in the integration of bodily and mental/affective spheres (soma and psyche) may lead to narcissistic pathology at best and self fragmentation as worst (Winnicott, 1949; 1960b). Due to a premature breakdown of the infant's developmental need for the illusion that he/she creates mother and mother's environmental provisions, a dissociative process sets in (i.e., something is concretely the thing itself, one thing or the other). The hallmark of symbolic capacity, to represent one thing by another, to consider another perspective, is compromised. This is a familiar enough event in clinical practice, when the "as if" experience of the transference breaks down, fails to develop, or is absent (i.e., only external and concrete versus symbolic, and containing some internal referent and meaning).

Winnicott (1963b) described a kind of compliant communication typical of the "false self" as a central pathological split between the subjective and objective object, noting that this communication is with the object as external (i.e., concrete and devoid of internal representation). He saw this as a precocious (not a gradual) development that should ideally emerge around good enough mothering and a solid internalisation of related holding-soothing functions. Instead, due to early impingements and environmental failures, a false-self develops. In this pathologic adaptation, the false-self complies in order to manage impingements from the external object, and to protect the core self, defensively separated in a form of private communication. (This is not to be confused with a healthy, private non-communicating core of the self that is central to authentic existence.) This pathological core was conceptualised as a more cordoned-off self, involved in what Winnicott called "cul-de-sac" communication—a more defensive and private communication in the realm of the subjective self. Winnicott expanded and organised these ideas later in his paper *Thinking and Symbol Formation* (1968) that described this precocious ego development and adaptation in ways that echo current ideas about the development (or failed development) of mentalisation (Fonagy & Target, 2007); Winnicott (1968) believed that due to maternal failure, an "inadequacy in the mother's attitude", the infant's "need for thinking becomes stepped up ... and strained as a function or acquires a new function" (p. 213).

We could consider this type of derailed communication and false-self development as representing a more schizoid mode, a self-object fantasy of care, reflection, and responsiveness of the environment and/or object mother who is available in ways that are (again) within one's omnipotent control (with the self precociously fabricating the maternal portion of the early object subjectively perceived). In this framework, the distinction between subjective and objective is potentially blurred or compromised; the related capacity for a symbolising process (i.e., that something might represent something else) is also poorly formed or compromised by a kind of premature and inauthentic articulation of the subjective self.

It is an essential feature of analytic process (however conceived) that traumatic failures and adaptive (defensive) manoeuvres are re-created via the transference as transitional space—from a Winnicottian perspective, a return to the situation of failure and hope for a new experience (1954). Some patients as described here may continue to need either or both the environment and object mothers as less than optimally internalised or integrated, and, in some cases, as profoundly split or dissociated functions, concretely expressed in the transitional organising experiences they bring to the analytic space. The gradual articulation of these transitional organising experiences may vary depending on the nature of the early disturbances and also particular environmental endowments, but the pull for the expression of these earliest experiences around these compromised core functions is similar: the opportunity for a resumption in the development of transitionality towards the developmental "use" of the object (Winnicott, 1971b) as separate, objectively perceived, and able to survive instinctual expressions of love and hate in a new object relationship (Loewald, 1960). Via the analyst as a facilitating presence, the analytic process supports the regressive experience needed for this new transitional experience.

There is a debate in recent analytic literature (Dunn, 1995; Ellman & Moskowitz, 2009; Fossage, 2005) about the relative effectiveness of verbal, interpretive interventions to reach early trauma and false-self development (seen by some as rooted in non-symbolic or pre-symbolic modes of experience), versus work focused on the intersubjective modes of experience (the realm of "implicit relational knowing" linked to early mutual dyadic regulation). It is also taken for granted that a capacity to hear and make use of transference or intrapsychic, conflict-focused interpretations (versus more concrete, affirmative, containing interventions) implies symbolising capacity. On the cusp of this capacity, however, described by Freedman and Russell (2003) as points of "incremental symbolization", there is a felt tension between concrete experiences and a nascent capacity to both feel and observe one's reactions as internal and symbolised in the transference. As implied here, these are always less than perfectly formed capacities; in that sense, like any early traumatic or conflictual configuration, they are prone to be repeated as a fixity of contemporary existence and a press for expression in analytic process as an intermediate (transitional) area.

Clinical experience suggests that the capacity to symbolise, whether conceptualised as defensively absent due to conflict, not encoded due to primitive anxieties (Bass, 2002; Freedman, 2002) or a function of deficits based in traumatic experiences (Silverman, 2002), is never entirely absent. It is useful to consider that Winnicott's notion of the role of the mother's adaptive capacity to regress to her infant's needs, also included the mother's higher ego functioning as mediating presence to both protect from impingements and also to optimally fail her infant's illusion of perfect attunement with mother as part of the self.

Considering such moments of potential transformation in clinical process from the perspective of Winnicott's construct of the transitional realm may help to capture both the intersubjective aspects of experience and the unique internal structures of patient and analyst. From this vantage point, it is the analyst's capacity for empathic attunement (as a kind of adaptive, creative regression in the service of the analytic ego) as well as adaptive movements to and from higher levels of internal structure (in sync with the patient's varying levels of psychic organisation) that mediates and bridges movements from non-symbolic, concrete experience towards symbolisation of transference experience (see Akhtar, 2002 and Kilingmo, 1989, for examples of an oscillating analytic technique from this perspective). These notions were elaborated by Loewald (1960) in his conceptualisation of the need for transference experience via the analyst's role as new object, in order to put words (i.e., symbolic structure, meaning) to what had been unorganised and compromised in early experience—in some sense related to what Bollas has referred to as the unthought known (1987) and Fonagy and Target (2007) describe as unmentalised experiences.

An emergent transitional organising experience may first be noted as a shift in the clinical atmosphere, a more deeply felt affective presence, or tension around mutual engagement such as a willingness to play or not (i.e., a more deadened or aggressively avoided, concrete holding onto experience versus a consideration of symbolic connections in the transference). In the perspective presented here, such clinical moments (in which the analyst's adaptive capacity for attunement to and articulation of his/her own as well as the patient's concrete, psychosomatic, and emergent unconscious fantasies) hold the potential for transformation towards greater symbolisation of experience. This way of thinking about clinical process is rooted both in Freud's (1914g) description of transference as playground, with the analytic space as intermediate area "between illness and real life ..." (p. 154), and Winnicott's crystallisation of Freud's notion with his creation of a construct, the transitional realm, to capture this as yet unarticulated area of human experience, between internal and external, between structured and intersubjective experience.

Aspects of the transitional realm have been utilised in a number of convergent ways as a conceptual tool to describe the emergence of such potential transformative shifts in the symbolisation of experience in analytic process. For example, Grunes (1984) referred to the importance of the analyst's adaptive capacity to enter states of "empathic permeability" in which mutual interpenetration between patient and analyst serves to capture emergent unconscious processes. In a similar way, Steingart (1998) noted that the analyst's mental state should ideally become emotionally arranged so as to foster the unfolding of the patient's repetition compulsion (p. 162) and to become receptive to communications within and between the dyad. Bollas (2001) seems to capture the interface around these positions in his reference to such states of intersubjectivity as a unique style of relating of the "Freudian pair", situated between the patient's free associations and the analyst's free associations, that "transfers the patient's unconscious contents to the psychoanalyst's unconscious organization" (p. 98).

Andre Green's (1987, 1987) construct of the "analytic object" (affective and bodily experiences situated between patient and analyst that become the object of analytic awareness and understanding) furthers the conceptualisation of the transitional realm as a joint or intersubjective creation of analyst and patient situated in intermediate space. Ogden's (1994) related construct of the "analytic third" is the experience of being simultaneously within and outside the intersubjectivity of the analyst and analysands. His notion of "interpretive action" (more palpable aspects of transference-interpretation that evolve from mutual intersubjective experiences in the analytic third) are interventions that serve as transitional phenomena and are facilitative of symbolisation. Freedman (1985, 1994, 2003, 2009) has described such nodal moments within the analytic process as shifts in transitional cycles of disruptive enactment, incremental movement, and transformation along a continuum of desymbolisation—symbolisation.

While virtually every psychoanalytic school now subscribes to some form of mutual influence between patient and analyst, there remains a range of acknowledgement and emphasis on the unique internal structures of patient and analyst and opinion on the degree to which these subjectivities can be objectively observed, adaptively negotiated, or even interpreted in the transference-countertransference (Dunn, 1995; Fossage, 2005). The burgeoning literature on intersubjectivity in the analytic process considers the analyst's influence and contribution as ranging from countertransference and enactments to "co-constructions" of content and experiences with the patient, seen as both dominating and moving the analytic process. Gentile (2007) offered an important reminder, however, about the tendency of contemporary intersubjectivity theorists to view the co-constructed aspects of analytic process as central as opposed to on a continuum that takes both subjectivity (psychic reality) and material reality into account (as described by Freud and later by Winnicott and implied in the view presented here).

Movements from concreteness to symbolising space via transitional organising experience

Compromised development of transitionality, viewed as based in early trauma and developmental failure, may emerge in analytic process in myriad ways. For some patients, more concrete objects, substances, the analyst him or herself, or some feature of the analytic milieu may come to serve this purpose; for others, some conscious or more unconscious self-representations or self/object fantasies may be operative and suggest a potential for shifts in symbolic capacity. These various shapes undoubtedly emerge in the dyad via the transference–countertransference. While such clinical presentations suggest a clinging to phenomena within the transitional realm to manage states of self-fragmentation and narcissistic vulnerability related to early trauma and developmental failure, analytic process in the neurotic-conflictual realm may also become organised at phases around aspects of transitionality (e.g., at termination). The fact that the analyst is a real presence (even for more symbolising patients) is confirmed by most patients' environmental as well as object needs, and ongoing use of transitional phenomena, however subtle or undetected, and are therefore always in the transference mix. It seems useful to recall Winnicott's (1951) reminder that something as subtle as a familiar sound or touch might be used in transitional fashion and may go unnoticed by parents in the course of early development (and perhaps analogously, by analysts in the regression of analytic process). Freud (1912b) first noted that the transference also needs a point of connection to some concrete piece of reality in the analyst in order to articulate the "stereotype plate" already established in the mind of the person (p. 100), perhaps an early acknowledgement of the way in which material and psychic reality coexist in creative intermediate space (Frosch, 2002).

The transference–countertransference might then be viewed within this framework as representing two (often intermingled) poles—the environment mother and the object mother, depending upon the degree to which compromised and/or unintegrated structural and intersubjective aspects are emergent via the transitional organising experience in the analytic process. It is the analyst's observational capacity, as well as attunement, empathic resonance, and intersubjective experiences, that help elucidate and articulate these experiences in the move towards symbolising space via the dyad.

In the following vignettes (Cancelmo, 2009, pp. 12–15), transitional organising experience emerged from the perspective of the two poles noted above. For Ms A, the analyst appeared to be used concretely, more as environment mother, yet also elaborated in fantasy, as an idealised but prosthetic (external) substitute for an early maternal failure. For Mr B, the early maternal failure had likely been compensated for by a masochistic but secretly grandiose fantasy of a self-object relationship of perfect "Christ-like" attunement to and with the object mother. Presented here[5] are moments where such organising and potentially transformative experiences emerged in the transference–countertransference via emotional resonance and related intersubjective experiences, but also as observed and articulated (and eventually interpreted) by the analyst.

Vignette: shifts in the use of the analyst as transitional organising experience

Ms A, an exquisitely controlled woman in her late forties, is moving reluctantly towards the realisation that an authentic life can only be lived without her constant pressured focus on gaining praise and adulation from others. She has laboured since her earliest memory in this way and feels "a high" (what she calls her "addiction") whenever evaluated by others as the smartest, the most competent, the most generous. She has become increasingly dissatisfied with this false-self life, devoid of spontaneity; however, without it, she feels empty and panicked, and drawn back to her compulsion to please. She says lately, "It's an illusion I delude myself with."

After the August break, I had returned with a beard—something contemplated for several years, but typically dismissed due to concerns about how *she* might respond to the change. This particular year, none of this material emerged beforehand for either Ms A or for me. While I had thought about my patients' reactions in general, she did not come to my mind, specifically. August breaks usually brought her concerns that she would forget our work, or that I would forget her, lose track of her; in her mind, we both suffered from problems with constancy and mentalisation.

Several days go by as we begin again. She makes no mention. I hear nothing derivative. Then she comes in late and for the first time, she does not apologise or agonise over her transgression. She tells me "nothing" is in her head; "I've stopped dead in the middle of my analysis." She feels empty—her worst fear realised, now that she is less focused on pleasing others and basking in their praise (both real and fantasised). She says, "Last night I had the thought—nothing is coming out of me. He is going to have a hard job now. He'll really hate me now." She admits to feeling stubborn, and I say to her: "So we're stuck here *together*."

She agrees. She shifts her carefully composed posture on the couch (a rare event). I am aware of feeling something deadened has come alive. In my reverie, she feels to me suddenly womanly and vibrant. Then an unusually long silence ensues. She says she has nothing in her mind. I say maybe we might consider that her angry feelings had scared her, and she pushed out any thought. She blurts out, uncharacteristically angry for her:

"I didn't even recognise you when you came back—that beard—you're like a different person I all of a sudden never knew. Then, who cares anyway, it's your business, who cares about your vacation, your wife, your children, your reasons for growing a beard. I know it's crazy, but it's just how I feel! I expected I could leave here eventually, and then if I came back everything would be the same, you would look exactly as I remember" (p. 14).

She connected this change in my appearance to loss of her use of me as someone who would cherish her perfection, and ultimately, to a new memory of a mother preoccupied with her new baby brother who was ill for many weeks after his birth. She notes that according to family lore, she stayed with relatives nearby while mother tended to him. When Ms A returned home, she was electively mute towards mother for days.

Dynamic formulation

On one hand, this clinical sequence could be viewed simply as an angry transference reaction, an instance of countertransference, or even an enactment. While such familiar dynamic constellations were all likely participants in this moment in the dyad, I believe that these terms, used in isolation from Winnicott's construct, can sometimes fail to capture the richness of the clinical process over time. I see these familiar dynamic constellations more broadly here as articulating movement in the transitional realm, a transitional organising experience, reflecting shifts towards higher levels of symbolisation via the transference as object relational experience.

Ms A, the child of a chronically unavailable mother and an intellectually demanding father, had created an idealised parental figure in her ego ideal that she felt "addicted" to (her words) for regulation of good feeling via a false-self. Ms A's concrete use of me in this way came to a crisis point in the transference–countertransference (as a transitional organising experience) due to this change in my real, actual, external appearance (i.e., analogous to an alteration of the transitional object).

In this change I had, like mother, not thought of her but rather thought of myself, my family. She had been reluctant to give me up as an idealised source of narcissistic supplies but experienced me as fully beyond her defensive omnipotent control.

My reference to a shared experience (via my countertransference attunement), in retrospect, addressed her worst fear—that her aggressiveness could not be contained and would be felt by me and retaliated; she was now able to risk expression of her anger in cutting me off, throwing me away, and I was there to receive and survive her aggression.

She could have filled the hour in a way she felt might please me, but gave this false-self mode of pathological transitional experience up. It is interesting to note here the physicality, the shift in posture, and the sense of embodiment felt in the countertransference, as a more creative use of personal space on the couch; this could be viewed as a move towards integration of psyche and soma that parallels her shift towards authentic expression of feeling and a more symbolised transference experience.

It felt to her that I had disrupted her illusion of being fed by me due to the change, the forgetting to consider her, yet she had not been so fearful of our separation either. The new awareness of this change in her was triggered by something outside (my appearance) but also something increasingly inside (her internal sense that she no longer wanted, needed constant praise and idealisation to feel full), and in the dyad, my internal experience of her as able to give up something real and addictive in the transference–countertransference (my not thinking of her specifically). Again, while my stance could also be considered a countertransference role responsiveness over time (Sandler, 1976), that view alone fails to capture the empathic attunement ("timing and tact") to keep my personal needs and wishes out until a readiness was sensed (an analytic co-construction outside conscious awareness) for an interpretive shift due to structural changes.

Vignette: negotiating the subjective/objective paradox
as transitional organising experience

Mr B, described here in the middle phase of a four times per week analysis, exemplifies a type of repetition of pathological adaptations and resulting compromised transitionality as noted in his transference experience. He had begun to articulate an unconscious fantasy of self as the suffering Christ, as noted in descriptions of the pain, agony, and ecstasy of his "maso*christic*" (his slip) enslavements to others, his Christ-like but grandiose and omnipotent compensatory fantasy of offering his life for the care of others in a state of perfect attunement.

Here he is in a typical repetitive mode, his private struggles to see me as other than the archaic, pathological self-with-object (Stern, 1985), now aired via the transference as his capacity for perfect attunement broke down. Talking to him about this helps elucidate, in fits and starts, a core dilemma that likely interfered with basic aspects of his early structuralisation, yet provides a "reliable" enslavement, a pathological transitional organising experience he brings to the analytic process. ("Pathological" in this context also refers to his experience of the new object in the transference as meagre in comparison to the toxic, enduring and familiar, yet secure old object of failure, who he tended to at his own expense and managed with a compensatory grandiose fantasy.) The emergence and painstaking working through of his conviction that his mind cannot be his outside enslaved connection to the other, can be seen in my view here as a pathological transitional space that is paradoxically a painful island of safety.

Mr B: I'm late today, so I'm feeling not here ... like I spoiled it so what's the point? ... I can feel myself on the surface of things, distant but I'm tied into you at the same time .... It all feels disjointed ... the questions keep coming ...why am I here? ... who is this for? I'm tied up with you and resisting at the same time. Had a similar feeling with Dee [his girlfriend] this morning ... I got her text message—she was on her blackberry, so I know she's right there, so it was nice and immediate, right there to me, but it feels like a demand to respond to her ... I can't have my own good feeling because hers takes over. She says she liked how I looked while shaving this morning; she said she was looking forward to the weekend. I feel I can't be free in the midst of her need for me ... no way I can do my thing ... have to respond to her wish to be with me .... I feel enslaved by her wanting me even though I want her ... she has to take precedence. I can only have this dialogue in my head not in reality with C ... can't risk the exposure.

I'm telling you all this right now … and it feels like you're not here … like I am talking to myself and hearing about myself … presumably you are the audience, so you must be here but you're not here. I can talk but it seems unreal.

A: You have some sense I exist, as an audience, but you need to leave me out of the equation, so maybe you don't feel caught up with a sense of pressure and demand you'll feel nothing that I am here listening even though you are late … maybe you fear using me here because you will end up feeling used, and tending to me, so the price is feeling unreal.

Mr B: I can't navigate this with you … with Dee … like in the triangle with my mother and father. Can't have one if I'm aligned with the other … it's the 'Vulcan mind meld'[6]; if I'm close and connected, I'm inside their thoughts and needs, they become mine, but then where am I?

I feel like that right now … F—YOU!! [with anger]; … I don't want to have to be present … it's painful to take the space for myself and then in the same breath feel doomed to regret it … I will end up having to lose something. [tearfully] … I had no right to let that out … that anger and frustration. You only let me hear back what I've been saying. I see that you are alive here and I register for you, I have an impact on you here when I'm not present. But you don't seem to mind, to begrudge me. I hear you but I see my mother's angry face, the scowl and then the dead absence, the silence in the house, the icy removal. … It feels hopeless … I know I'm rejecting your help right now when I say that … It always comes back to this … has it changed? Do I want it to change? I remember your old office … saying how hopeless I felt … this feels not so bottled up, not so hopeless, but I can't fully give that to you … I imagine you could hold it against me and expect repayment for helping get to a less hopeless place … a constant debt to repay so I get caught up in my enslavement again … it is something I know, it's reliable.

Dynamic formulation

I feel a familiar struggle in the countertransference, a gut feeling, like a rock lodged inside my chest, a concrete presence and sensation he has described to me when feeling stuck with his attachment to mother as an immovable presence, a dead weight he felt destined to move around in order to keep her (and him) alive. Again he is here and not here, now dead weight to me, as if collaborating but not, making me ineffectual, turning me into a self like his, a concordant identification (Racker, 1953) in which we both cannot feel autonomous and still connected. The reconstruction via the transference–countertransference of this basic bind around negotiating subjectivity and objectivity appears to move via his aggression; I feel it, and then he becomes aware of feeling it, and my presence in the face of it, as well as its impact on me and on him, and some oscillation is felt between us that suggests a nascent transition towards a more objective stance—a moment of transitional organising experience in the dyad. It is the "holding onto" that perpetuates a pathological transitional mode. His awareness of this via the exchange in the transference helps mobilise the expression of aggression to self and other (the analyst in the transference). This moment contains much more than aggression-frustration and reflects a complex situation of repetition and adhesive masochistic and sadistic attachment that is noted via the dyadic experience, one unlike the psychic reality of his earliest structuralisations in the transitional mode. It is symbolisation *in statu nascendi*, a nascent capacity to observe and feel this experience as (also) transference and not merely a painful repetition. It is uncanny to note that the blackberry technology takes on both transitional and persecutory qualities, and he becomes aware of the holding-soothing aspects in a new way ("… I know she's right there … it was nice and immediate, right there to me, but it feels like a demand to respond to her …").

Summary

This chapter considers the organisational and transformational power of Winnicott's construct of the transitional realm to both elucidate and facilitate movements towards greater symbolisation—referred to here as *transitional organising experience*. This perspective on Winnicott's work suggests that the essential developmental tasks that are the hallmark of transitionality (a sorting-out of a separate yet interdependent self with a mind of one's own, negotiating the subtleties of subjectivity and objectivity, the development of creative space for symbolic experience), less than optimally formed due to early impingements and compromised internalisations, may come to organise analytic process for such patients. These less than optimal structuralisations and compromised intersubjective capacities inevitably press for expression in the regressive experience of analysis as intermediate space via the transference–countertransference. Such moments are often felt clinically as impasse and stalemates, states of concreteness, and compromised symbolic capacity. The particular manifestation of these compromised structural and intersubjective capacities is, of course, unique and varies for each patient according to particular emotional endowment, early environmental experience, and the transference–countertransference that inevitably develops. There may be, however, some common elements as implied in Winnicott's construct and suggested by the clinical vignettes presented here, for example: a) a subjective-objective dilemma which may coalesce around a false-self, b) a fantasy of self-care, either in regressive or defensive form (as in a self-object dependency, or a pathological grandiose self), and c) a tendency towards a fixity of experience, an attachment that encapsulates both a repetition of the trauma and a hope for a higher level of structuralisation.

As conceptualised here, moments of transitional organising experience are, by their very nature, an admixture of concrete and symbolic experiences. They present a potential for the transformation of structural and intersubjective capacities, in particular, for some of our more challenging patients with compromised internalisations and pathological organisations based in early disturbances. Via the analyst's attunement to the possibility for a re-experiencing and reorganising of pathological transitional modes and related compromised symbolic capacities (versus a more unitary clinical focus on such difficulty as merely structural "resistance"), a resumption of development in symbolising space via the analytic process may be possible.

References

Abram, J. (1997). *The Language of Winnicott*. Northvale, NJ: Jason Aronson.
Adler, G. (1989). Transitional phenomena, projective identification, and the essential ambiguity of the psychoanalytic situation. *Psychoanalytic Quarterly*, 58: 81–104.
Akhtar, S. (2002). From schisms through synthesis to informed oscillation: An attempt at integrating some diverse aspects of psychoanalytic technique. *Psychoanalytic Quarterly*, 64: 265–288.

Aron, L. (2006). Analytic impasse and the third: Clinical implications of intersubjectivity theory. *International Journal of Psychoanalysis, 87*: 349–368.

Bach, S. (1984). Perspectives on Self and Object. *Psychoanaltyic Review, 71*: 145–168.

Bass, A. (2002). Desymbolization in the third area. In: R. Lasky (Ed.), *Symbolization and Desymbolization: Essays in Honor of Norbert Freedman.* New York: Other Press.

Bollas, C. (1979). The transformational object. *International Journal of Psychoanalysis, 60*: 97–107.

Bollas, C. (1987). *The Shadow of the Object. Psychoanalysis of the Unthought Known.* New York: Columbia University Press.

Bollas, C. (1993). An interview with Christopher Bollas. *Psychoanalytic Dialogues, 3*: 401–430.

Bollas, C. (2001). Freudian intersubjectivity: Commentary on paper by Julie Gerhardt and Annie Sweetnam. *Psychoanalytic Dialogues, 11*: 93–195.

Bolognini, S. (2004). Intrapsychic-Interpsychic. *International Journal of Psychoanalysis, 85*: 337–358.

Brandchaft, B. (2007). Systems of pathological accommodation and change in analysis. *Psychoanalytic Psychology, 24*: 667–687.

Brody, S. (1980). Transitional objects: Idealization of a phenomenon. *Psychoanalytic Quarterly, 49*: 561–605.

Cancelmo, J. A. (2009). The role of the transitional realm as an organizer of analytic process: Transitional organizing experience. *Psychoanalytic Psychology, 26*: 2–25.

Coppolillo, H. P. (1967). Maturational aspects of transitional phenomena. *International Journal of Psychoanalysis, 48*: 237–246.

Dunn, J. (1995). Intersubjectivity in psychoanalysis: A critical review. *International Journal of Psychoanalysis, 76*: 723–738.

Ellman, S. J. (2010). *When Theories Touch.* London: Karnac.

Ellman, S. J. & Moskowitz, M. (2009). A study of the Boston Change Process Study Group. *Psychoanalytic Dialogues, 18*: 812–837.

Fossage, J. L. (2005). The explicit and implicit domains in psychoanalytic change. *Psychoanalytic Inquiry, 25*: 516–539.

Freedman, N. (1985). The concept of transformation in psychoanalysis. *Psychoanalytic Psychology, 4*: 317–339.

Freedman, N. (1994). More on transformation: Enactments in psychoanalytic space. In: A. K. Richards & A. D. Richards (Eds.), *Essays in Honor of Martin S. Bergmann.* Madison, CT: International Universities Press.

Freedman, N. & Russell, J. (2003). Symbolization of the analytic discourse. *Psychoanalysis and Contemporary Thought, 26*: 39–87.

Freud, S. (1912b). The dynamics of transference. *S. E., 12*: 97–108. London: Hogarth.

Freud, S. (1914g). Remembering, repeating and working through. *S. E., 12*: 145–157. London: Hogarth.

Freud, S. (1923b). *The Ego and the Id. S. E., 19*: 3–68. London: Hogarth.

Frosch, A. (2002). Transference: Psychic reality and material reality. *Psychoanalytic Psychology, 19*: 603–633.

Gentile, J. (2007). Wrestling with matter: Origins of intersubjectivity. *Psychoanalytic*.

Green, A. (1978). Potential space in psychoanalysis: The object in the setting. In: *Between Reality and Fantasy*. Northvale, NJ: Jason Aronson.

Green, A. (1987). *On private madness*. New York: International Universities Press. *Quarterly, 76*: 547–582.

Grunes, M. (1984). The therapeutic object relationship. *Psychoanalytic Review, 71*: 123–143.

Killingmo, B. (1989). Conflict and deficit: Implications for technique. *International Journal of Psychoanalysis, 70*: 65–79.

Kohut, H. (1971). *The Analysis of the Self*. New York: International Universities Press.

Loewald, H. (1960). On the therapeutic action of psychoanalysis. In: *Papers on Psychoanalysis*. New Haven, CT: Yale University Press.

Loewald, H. (1978). Instinct theory, object relations, and psychic structure formation. In: *Papers on Psychoanalysis*. New Haven, CT: Yale University Press, 1980.

Ogden, T. (1994). *Subjects of Analysis*. Northvale, NJ: Jason Aronson.

Racker, H. (1953). A contribution to the problem of countertransference. *International Journal of Psychoanalysis, 34*: 314–324.

Sandler, J. (1976). Countertransference and role-responsiveness. *International Review of Psycho-Analysis, 3*: 43–47.

Sanville, J. (1991). *The Playground of Psychoanalytic Therapy*. Hillsdale, NJ: Analytic Press.

Silverman, D. (2002). The refractoriness of the desymbolizing function. In: R. Lasky (Ed.), *Symbolization and Desymbolization: Essays in Honor of Norbert Freedman*. New York: Other Press.

Steiner, J. (1993). *Psychic Retreats: Pathological Organizations in Psychotic, Neurotic, and Borderline Patients*. London: Routledge.

Steingart, I. (1995). *A Thing Apart*. Northvale, NJ: Jason Aronson.

Steingart, I. (1998). A contemporary-classical Freudian views the current conceptual scene. In: C. S. Ellman, S. Grand, M. Silvan & S. J. Ellman (Eds.), *The Modern Freudians: Contemporary Psychoanalytic Technique*. Northvale, NJ: Jason Aronson.

Van der Kolk, B. (1989). The compulsion to repeat the trauma: Re-enactment, re-victimization, and masochism. *Psychiatric Clinics of North America, 12*: 389–410.

Winnicott, D. W. (1949). Mind and its relation to the psyche-soma. In: *Through Paediatrics to Psycho-analysis*. New York: Basic.

Winnicott, D. W. (1951). Transitional objects and transitional phenomena. In: *Through Paediatrics to Psycho-analysis*. New York: Basic.

Winnicott, D. W. (1954). The depressive position in normal emotional development. In: *Through Paediatrics to Psycho-analysis*. New York: Basic.

Winnicott, D. W. (1960a). The theory of the parent-infant relationship. In: *The Maturational Processes and the Facilitating Environment*. Madison, CT: International Universities Press.

Winnicott, D. W. (1960b). Ego distortion in terms of true and false self. In: *The Maturational Processes and the Facilitating Environment*. Madison, CT: International Universities Press.

Winnicott, D. W. (1963a). The development of the capacity for concern. In: *The maturational processes and the facilitating environment*. Madison, CT: International Universities Press.

Winnicott, D. W. (1963b). From dependence to towards independence in the development of the individual. In: *The maturational processes and the facilitating environment*. Madison, CT: International Universities Press.

Winnicott, D. W. (1968). Thinking and symbol formation. In: *Psychoanalytic explorations*. C. Winnicott, R. Shepard and M. Davis, Eds. Boston: Harvard University. Press.

Winnicott, D. W. (1971b). Mirror-role of mother and family and child development. In: *Playing and reality*. New York: Basic Books.

Notes

1. The term *transitional realm* is used to describe the wide applications and extensions of Winnicott's construct of the intermediate area of experience (including transitional space and potential space) as well as the various developmental markers that signify its development (i.e., transitional phenomena and the transitional object). Brody (1980) noted that this conceptual umbrella has been used in the literature (e.g., Abram, 1997; Coppolillo, 1967) because of the inherent vagueness (which some might call the paradoxical, illusory, and creative quality) of Winnicott's construct.

2. Transitionality refers here to an optimal capacity, crystallised in the transitional phase, that allows for the full experience of the creative and adaptive potentials that live between illusion and reality, an immersion

in transitional space as interpsychic experience between self and other (Bolognini, 2004), and intersubjective space where ownership of creativity is also co-constructed (Aron, 2006). In the view offered here, these capacities rest on the secure developmental achievement of self and other definition, separation, and internalisation (i.e., an intrapsychic structure), towards which there is an inherent organising thrust (Loewald, 1960).

3. I refer broadly here to fantasies, enactments, and adhesive attachments to and transformations of self and object representations that may emerge in the transference–countertransference and may come to serve as transitional organising experiences.

4. Winnicott used the terms transitional phenomena and transitional object both in distinct ways and synonymously between 1951 and 1971 (a) to imply a developmental sequence from early tactile and sensory processes as transitional phenomena that proceed and blend into the transitional object and its usage, (b) to denote phenomena subsequent to the period of the transitional object, such as the older child's use of a tune or repertoire of songs, to developmental moves towards phenomena in the area of cultural and religious experiences, and (c) to create a conceptual umbrella, "transitional phenomena" as a designation of all phenomena (including the transitional object) within the intermediate area of experience.

5. Copyright © 2009 by the American Psychological Association. Adapted with permission.

6. The "Vulcan Mind Meld" (http://www.memory-alpha.org) refers to the TV series Star Trek and a lead character, Spock, who can take on the mind of the other, a sharing of consciousness between two parties as a function of extraordinary cognitive capacity. There is an inherent risk of loss of one's own identity in the procedure and its aftermath. Mr B's metaphor captures this aspect of his precocious capacity for attunement to the other and the subjective-objective blurring that paradoxically remains his dilemma.

CHAPTER FOUR

Enactment: opportunity for symbolising trauma

Paula L. Ellman and Nancy R. Goodman

While psychoanalysis, by tradition, has emphasised the medium of thought and fantasy, the call to action likewise takes place continuously in psychoanalytic treatment (Loewald, 1975), sometimes in subtle tones and nuanced body movements or startling unexpected interactions. Over the past twenty years, the term enactment has been developing as a way to identify a stream of activity and to acknowledge the richness of communication contained in the action process. These evocative action sequences involve analysand and analyst, and are frequently motivated by the analysand's traumatic history, bypassing the symbolic verbal narrative, and making its way into the nonverbal transference/countertransference arena. Within the analytic dyad, the analysis of enactment leads to the symbolisation of trauma and the multiple meanings it has in psychic life.

In psychoanalysis, analysts often find that there is a drama by reflecting on the role they have been drawn into playing (Sandler, 1976). In this way, therapeutic listening catches up with what has been taking place and becomes recognised after the fact (Goodman et al., 1993). It is through countertransference awareness (Ellman, P., 1998; Ellman, S. & Moskowitz, 1998; Freedman, Barroso, Bucci & Grand, 1978; Jacobs, 1986; Tyson & Renik, 1986) that the analyst comes to know the enactment and finds the story of what has been repressed or never known. Jacobs first introduced the concept of enactment in 1986 in a paper entitled, "Countertransference Enactments". Attention to the idea of enactment has led psychoanalysts to clarify the existence of a new road to the unconscious augmenting Freud's royal road of dream imagery. Chused (1991) reported that psychoanalysts involved in a 1989 panel discussion on enactment "... agreed that enactments in analysis are inevitable ..." and wondered, "... whether and how enactments could beneficially contribute to the analytic process ..." (p. 615). In their edited book, *Enactment: Toward a New Approach in the Therapeutic Relationship*, Ellman, S. and Moskowitz (1998) brought together historic and contemporary articles addressing the enactment process, breaking barriers by allowing for the discussion of analytic interactions playing out unconscious matters. At the same time, Katz (1998) offered a review of the "enacted dimension of the analytic process" where transference is not just represented on a verbally symbolised level. Enactment is a bridge term "... subsuming both the overt patient-analyst interaction and the underlying unconscious fantasies being actualised ..." (p. 1153).

The enactments arising from traumas often bypass symbolic verbal narrative and are communicated through action. The concept of "concreteness" (Bass, 1997) offers further definition of the nature of psychic functioning in enactment. With regard to the place of trauma in the mind, concreteness results from the overwhelming affects not available to symbolisation. Stern (1983) developed the idea of "... unformulated experience ... the unformulated is a conglomeration not yet knowable in the separate and definable of language" and "is composed of vague tendencies ... which can be shaped and articulated .... Meaning becomes creation ..." (p. 72). In his work with survivors of mass trauma including Holocaust survivors, Laub (1992) identified "holes" in the mind. Likewise, Kogan (2007), in her treatment of children of Holocaust survivors, noted that enactments were the first steps to coming to know. Lear (2000) wrote of a lack of content accompanying "deepest forms of human helplessness" that he described as "quantity without quality" (p. 109). When the psyche is overwhelmed with affect, meaning may not yet exist since language may not be available to symbolise the trauma. The concreteness indicates an event existing where internal fantasy and external reality are not distinguishable. Hanna Segal wrote of the "symbol equation" (1957) "... where there is non-differentiation between the thing symbolised and the symbol ... this is part of a disturbance in the relationship between the ego and the object ..." (p. 393).

Once a concrete enactment is identified within transference/counter-transferance configurations, symbolisation begins. Naming the affects in interaction brings clarity and further differentiation to traumatic experience and to the associated unconscious fantasies. Central to the transformation into symbolisation is the analytic dyad affording the contextual meaning for the symbol. The enactment is the event where unformulated experience is perched and ready for translation into a language having symbolic meaning in the mutuality of the dyad.

The authors present two diverse analyses so as to further clarify how analysing enactment provides for movement from concreteness to symbolisation, thereby bringing about a more meaningful understanding of the unfolding psychic reality. One case demonstrates how trauma can come to be expressed and understood through an ongoing enactment related to a pervasive character structure that Goodman (1998) referred to as "character enactment". In the course of the patient's analysis, language was used in a concrete way to disavow the communication potential of words and analytic vitality. Speaking became a means of controlling the analyst's existence through the creation of a mood of deadness. In the deadness of the enactment resided the patient's unconscious certainty that contact brings traumatic annihilation, recapitulating an early object relationship. The patient attempted to feel alive by ridding himself of the terror that separateness brings and his sense of deficiency over which he despaired. The second case involves a dramatic interaction of a hug with the analyst, followed over the next four years with reaching out many times to touch the analyst. The enactments were representations of interactions holding overwhelming affects of terror and helplessness belonging to traumatic situations that had never been symbolised in the analysand's mind. The event of the "hug" became the centrepiece of analytic work leading to understanding of the impact of traumatic events and their sequelae. Then, the analysis was able to identify the network of fantasies about seduction, surrender, and death that had become part of the patient's psychic reality and now were part of the psychic reality of the treatment. The two cases illustrate the relevance of trauma active in both discrete enactment events and in ongoing enactments related to character.

Case: Mr T

Mr T wanted an analysis because he was unassertive, was unable "to feel", and felt deficient. Early in the analysis, Mr T recounted memories without any apparent meaningful connection to his current state of mind or life. He found satisfaction in his claim that he was doing his analysis correctly by "free associating" and not censoring. He brought in dreams, not because he remembered them and was affectively attached to them, but because he had written them down. He told of events that he thought "should" stir him; he stated that he knew how he "should feel" but did not feel.

Mr T wanted the analyst to be fully "attuned", to feel what he feels as he feels it. To feel for herself, as his analyst, was not sufficient. Mr T associated his longing for attunement to his mother "raising me by the book", according to strict rules. He remembered minimal involvement with an unempathic stern mother and remote ineffective father. Mr T frequently returned to his memory of an event that he "supposed" to be traumatic and formative: the "trip to the institution". He had disobeyed, mother threatened to leave him at the nearby institution, he continued to disobey, and she drove him to the institution. The car ride created sheer panic for Mr T, as he begged his mother to take him home, believing in his impending abandonment. Upon arriving at the institution, she immediately returned home with him. The memory suggests a traumatic history of relatedness and attachment, and provided a way to understand the transference/countertransference of his using language to deaden the analysis and prevent contact. He could disable the analyst from driving the "analytic car" with its risks of destroying him and keep himself from having awareness of his terror of aggression and annihilation.

For the analyst, Mr T's words lost their vitality and prevented contact. The analyst felt she did not exist. At times, she felt a drugged sleepiness come over her as she saw herself as a helpless ineffectual mother or an inanimate object. An excerpt from an hour illustrates the patient's language and its power in evoking an ongoing enactment with the analyst. The "dead" mood that Mr T created in the analytic hour is apparent. The concept of "concreteness" brings further understanding to the functioning of Mr T's psyche in this ongoing enactment where language coupled with the absence of affect became an action to prevent contact. The action was the concrete expression of trauma, and as the traumatic meaning was not yet symbolised, action made for a distorted function of his language. In this session the patient's wish for a tape recorder serves as a condensation illustrating the patient's mechanistic approach to language that was used to create deadness with the analyst.

A Friday:

Patient: I would like to tape record Wednesday and Friday hours. I'd get back into where I left off, especially when the previous time is not present in my mind, like right now. It would help that sense that something is wrong with me; I'd retain a full sense of the previous hour.

Analyst: [Annoyed at his efforts to control with the intrusion of a machine, thereby feeling attacked in her analysing function.] You're feeling this is not satisfying and you're finding some way to overcome this feeling. [The analyst responds with just one possibility of meaning, facilitating the concreteness of the exchange. Another possible meaning not considered is that he is afraid people do not exist when they are apart.]

Patient: I don't seem to notice a strong feeling; I just thought taping would be advantageous. When I talk, it seems unproductive. It's not a strong feeling. I thought taping is a way to be more productive, not that I have unbearable, painful, or strong feelings. I always look for an edge. [Silence, patient falls asleep and snores. The patient here fends off the analyst and the analysis, and at the same time is expressing his feeling that he is falling off the abyss.]

Analyst: [Also feeling sleepy in response to the patient's opposition to the analyst's clarification.] Having an edge might help stave off the temptation to sleep. [Concrete.]

Patient: I think of sleeping as something else. It's just due to being tired on Fridays. The edge is to avoid hours when I think nothing is going on here, when I didn't see anything in a new light. I want to jump over those times, and get on a roll. What do you think?

Analyst: [Feeling helplessly ineffective, and believing that he truly does not want to know what she thinks.] What do you think you may be keeping out of analysis by recording it? [The analyst is concrete in speaking to one possible meaning and only a defensive one, thereby joining the patient in creating a deadness and an enactment of concreteness.]

Patient: What I'd be keeping out is not such a big thing. Maybe I don't give full weight to noticing that I feel something else. I would only use the recording to cut interference between hours. [Could the "interference" be about his being left at the institution; but the analyst did not see this meaning at this moment.]

Analyst: [Feeling irrelevant to him and the analysis, like she does with his writing notes after hours.] Like when you write down what you remember after each hour.

Patient: But it's better than writing it down. I don't want any of it to get lost. By taping, I'd not forget even a step, an insight. [The patient is terrified of losing the analyst but the analyst remains deaf to this communication.]

Analyst: [Thinking about transference in terms of the possible concerns he has about separating from her.] Anything else you are worried about getting lost?

Patient: Not so much the insight, but how I came to the insight. To capture the little steps leading up to its gradually unfolding. I'd listen to the tape before the next hour.

Analyst: As if no time elapsed.

Patient: Exactly, no time would elapse. It would be like a continuous two hours in a row.

Analyst: Like we would not be apart.

Patient: Of course that could be the meaning, but it doesn't strike me that way. I think of it like two separate tracks, like film spliced together while what happens day to day wouldn't throw the film off track.

Analyst: [Move from concreteness to contact.] And you could direct the film and not chance any frightening feeling.

Patient: Seems like I would want to continue a satisfying experience. It would be disappointing to not be able to have it, I'd forget it, and it is not alive anymore. [Here is the annihilation.] I am reminded of the meetings I lead. I need to prepare enough to get back the sense of excitement, aliveness.

Analyst: Is it hard to get that back, that aliveness?

Patient: Something is deficient in me; you imply that something is really going on here? One has to think about deficiency if one's arm is cut off. This could fit with re-creating the moment. I used to replay meetings in my mind. I wouldn't let them go. This morning the meeting was a good one, and I wanted to replay the little moments: someone says this, someone responds, it feels really good. But I know that the replaying is not productive and is only for my gratification.

Analyst: It feels important to be productive and fend off feeling deficient.

Patient: I would want to listen to the tape of the hour just before my next hour; and get that high state of feeling alive. It is a way I could perpetuate the sense of being alive.

Mr T's intellectualisation and splitting off of affect, both derivatives of his character, made for his mode of communication in this ongoing enactment of a mood of deadness. In the deadness Mr T disavowed the analyst's "otherness" and her vitality. The analyst's separateness in her analytic function represented a threat of despair for Mr T. He believed he fell asleep only because he was tired, not allowing for consideration of unconscious motivation. He wished to record hours only because of his memory "deficiency", not to stave off his "deadness". He disregarded any suggestion from the analyst of her separateness and of the symbolic meaning to these events. Likewise, Mr T demonstrated a fusion between his self and object representations in his relatively undifferentiated ego-ideal; he behaved "as though he was his own ego-ideal" (Reich, 1954). Mr T wanted to feel productive by recording the hour, thereby capturing the steps of his insight. He wanted to savour the exhilaration of his "productivity" by replaying an hour on tape, replaying his professional meeting in his mind, reviewing his steps towards an insight or professional success. Recording an hour served to disavow the differentiating effect of time as if analyst and patient were never parted. Mr T's conscious concern was his deadness and aliveness, his battle with his sense of "deficiency". To "feel good" through productivity and accomplishment, to "perpetuate the high state of feeling alive", Mr T engaged in an ongoing enactment of preventing separateness. He feared losing the analyst as she does not exist when they are apart and he feels deficient, dead and vulnerable. Overwhelming affects associated with the trauma of threatened and actual affective abandonments were not yet symbolised in language. Mr T's use of language as action, not as symbolic verbal narrative, moved the dyad into the enactment. The analyst's countertransferential concreteness was manifested in her interpreting the taping solely as a defence. The existence of multiple meanings was dead for both. She struggled with considering the patient's wish to take his analyst with him as she did not exist for him when they were apart. Both patient and analyst were caught in the terror of aggression and annihilation. The patient's effort was to fend off the analysis and keep the analyst with him so that both could continue to exist. The analyst was locked in her feeling of being kept out and shut down. As she experienced the patient's efforts to grip her, she freed herself from the deadness of mood, extracted herself from her concreteness, and asked "Is there anything else you are worried about losing?" It was then that the patient related the exhilaration of the merger fantasy, enacting a state of the dyad as not separate and distinct, and also denying contact to stave off the anticipated terror of annihilation.

Through recognition of the ongoing transference enactment, the derivatives of conflict around separation then became available to analysis, and involved Mr T's seeing his creation of this mood of deadness more directly. He said, "I am in a coffin," as he lay on the couch gazing ahead; or "I'm a rock on the ground as a stampede of animals trample over," "I am underwater and everything is motionless." Each hour Mr T hoped for something to happen; he yearned to create life, understanding, meaning, and invigoration. When he believed nothing happened, he left lifeless. He recalled times as the young boy sent to his room, alone, lifeless. Through his language, Mr T enacted the unconscious image of closing out the analyst and deadening the object relationship. Contact only meant annihilation. Not to be overlooked is the layering of Mr T's castration anxiety in his associations of having his arm cut off. Mr T was concretely caught between his longing to retain the good contact with the analyst, "wanting to replay the little moments", and his fear of losing hold of something precious to him.

The struggle for the analyst included the effort to extract herself from a concrete process and allow for multiple meanings in the patient's communications. Articulating the deadness of the enactment was the first step of the analyst entering the patient's inner world. Mr T's struggle to achieve his "sense of aliveness" came to be understood through the analyst/patient dyad's enactment as his dread of non-existence, annihilation, and his longing for contact and permanence. All roads led to Mr T's reconstruction of trauma as the terrorised child of a rigid, disengaged, and actively sadistic mother, thereby opening the way for Mr T's greater accessibility in his relations.

Case: Ms M

An enactment in the second year of Ms M's analysis brought to life major traumas related to childhood abandonments, sexual seductions and betrayals, and additionally the traumatic death of her infant son after birth. In the last session before the analyst's vacation, Ms M sat up from the couch, started to walk away, reached the door, and brought her hand to her head saying she just could not leave. As she told her analyst about feeling dizzy, she seemed to be folding to the floor. The analyst walked towards her, reaching out and Ms M collapsed into the analyst's arms. The analyst assisted the patient back to the couch and Ms M sat down. She thanked the analyst for helping her. The analyst sat in her chair and asked Ms M if she could put into words what was happening. She focused her gaze on the floor quietly speaking: "I don't know exactly. Everything was black and scary. I feel very very small, maybe a baby. My whole body feels strange like I'm not even me. I could not go. That is all I know. You did not push me away, you did not act angry, you let me cling to you as I hugged you and felt your caring for me as you held me up. I can trust that. I know you do not hate me. Now I can leave and I know I can remember you and your help."

Countertransference is often the catalyst by which enactments become identified and enter a symbolising process. There is a communication to the analyst that needs to be put into words. On vacation the analyst was aware of feeling relieved that her patient stated so clearly she could now tolerate the separation. The analyst recalled important hugs from her own grandmother that had felt life-saving as a child. She also felt annoyingly preoccupied with this treatment during her vacation. Along with the feeling of comfort and of nurturing was a sense of worry as the analyst wondered if this act of "helping" her patient was indeed a transgression and risked the treatment's viability. The analyst felt guilty. Maybe she had unconsciously stirred up this activity and caused a defect to enter the work. Labelling and symbolising her feelings and ideas helped, as did a renewed interest in psychoanalytic enactments. Ms M's psyche was overwhelmed in reaction to the summer separation and responded in the concrete actualisation of a collapse in body that the analyst also responded to in real action. Ms M. had acted out with the analyst the belief that she had to touch her analyst, emotionally and actually, and activated the analyst to show her responsiveness in order to be able to leave for three weeks. The concreteness in Ms M's psyche relating to unknown trauma and the analyst's response created the enactment. The intensity of the countertransference opened the way for understanding the multiply layered motivations for its creation.

After the summer vacation the patient spoke of her feeling of being accepted and held, and labelled the interaction with her analyst as "the hug" which was sustaining for her through the three-week separation. The concrete event of the enactment was now a symbol, an image, carrying meaning of referencing traumatic events and unconscious fantasies. What was compellingly repeated, in order to not know, entered a process of becoming known. As analyst and analysand viewed this sculpted image, affects, memories, and wishes entered the analytic work with intensity and conviction. Thoughts about "the hug" appeared to function for the patient as a safety zone containing the idea of her analyst's true concern for her. Simultaneously, it functioned as a fantasy construction leading to the uncovering of powerful affective experiences related to childhood betrayals and the loss of the baby who had never been touched or held. The feelings contained in the embrace led to the increasing availability of affects related to these major traumas of childhood and to the lack of a somatic bond with her infant. Her belief was that all good objects are destined to disappear. An array of deeply held unconscious ideas concerning her capacity to seduce and to murder emerged.

Sessions came alive as Ms M. spoke of traumatic events, not only as a reporter of fact, but as a way to communicate to and explore with her analyst. She first recalled a sense of closeness and security associated to hugs and caresses from the kitchen help and nursemaids of early childhood. She recalled the sensory memory of playing and looking at books in the crook of a tree behind the house. The capacity to experience the holding represented in "the hug" allowed the traumatic affects of early childhood to appear and be linked to her early life actualities. With this linking she came to know early overwhelming experiences related to abandonment and sexual arousal. Thus, the work at uncovering the derivatives that created "the hug" oscillated between finding ways to symbolise despair and to elucidate fantasies of merger with the analyst either through erotic ecstasy or through death.

The narrative of childhood emerged with increasing clarity as she put these traumatic affects into words. She sketched out in distilled and fragmented imagery various experiences of childhood where she felt psychic helplessness. She narrated being sent to boarding school in the mountains at the age of five after a sexual seduction by an older male cousin. She would be home only for summers from then on, often alone with her depressed, withdrawn, and suicidal alcoholic mother. Naps with her mother included arousing physical contact and intense shame and guilt. She conveyed the despair of her childhood with poetic words: "All I feel is cold, so much cold. I need to get close to you to feel warm. Where are my memories? I think of the tragedies on TV, the faces of starving children in Rwanda, almost dead, unable to wave flies away. That train ride to school, leaving, leaving, leaving … blank staring faces, trains in Nazi Germany taking people to death. I wished to be dead." There were painful memories about forbidden deeds. "Sometimes I would crawl into bed with another girl, we would warm each other. Maybe we were sexual: I had to feel alive and felt so guilty. Why was I sent away?" She was amazed that she could find ways to talk, and that she was not going to be sent away for what she feared and wished she could do with the analyst/mother.

A deep depression of early childhood and a desire to die were embedded in layers of erotic fantasies then present with the analyst. In her fantasies and recollections it was unclear who did what to whom, and what was pleasure and what was pain. In analysis she confronted what she was sure she could not face—the death of her baby and the ways she felt implicated because she had let herself trust a physician who, she knew, drank too much. While the actualities of this event were repressed, they continually appeared symbolically in repetitive patterns of birth, guilt, and death. She would abort creative projects, or if completed, she would bring terrible suffering upon herself. She had never touched nor held her infant son during the few hours he lived nor after he died. Her desire to hold her baby and her fear of being a "death" machine were also elements of the enacted "hug". She had almost no memory of the days after the baby's death and did not recall grief, but instead she felt elation at the thought of her infant in a safe pain-free place. Life and death, pleasure and pain, autonomy and submission were scrambled. She asked: "Who needs to be held, who did not get held, who died?" The analyst asked if the overwhelming need to make contact with the analyst contained knowledge of the need she had felt to hold her baby, to feel his form. Every time the analyst spoke to her about what it would feel like to hold him, she cried. The "hug" with her analyst led to articulation of what the baby would have felt like and a true somatically based experience of grief twenty years after the event. She became clearer with the details of what happened, more able to distinguish then from now, and less merged with the newborn and with her analyst.

Accompanying the discovery and symbolisation of these traumas were unconscious fantasies about her seductiveness and aggression. Her psyche used the "not knowing" of trauma to "not know" her own forbidden desires. She began to articulate her desire for more hugs, her desire to change the analytic situation. She and the analyst were able to understand how she wanted to do to the analyst what had been done to her. If she could seduce her analyst, then the analysis would never end, there would be no grief, and there would be an actual timeless forbidden embrace. If she died and did not thrive, she could make the analyst feel guilt and despair forever. She was able to speak of her desire to attack the analyst through seduction, and to induce in the analyst a state of feeling defective as she had felt from her mother's seductions. She wanted to have the analyst deliver a dead analysis; and like her, be a mother lost in grief. This capacity to recognise her own aggression was the final step in creating a symbolic narrative in the place of concrete re-enacted action sequences.

The actual hug entered the symbolic language of the analysis as something that had to be talked about, something that was felt about, something that related both to the past and to the here and now of the analysis. The analyst's unconscious mind entered a place of helpless terror that brought her into action with her patient. The relation of past to present contained in the terror and the symbolic representations related to trauma and to conflict became knowable through the actions. The analyst's first inklings about holding, comfort, seduction, and defect, and the analyst's ability to name these internal reactions portended what would come to be known in the analysand's mind. As the hug became a symbol and a connection to deep psychic experience, including Ms M's wish to create a defective merger with the analyst, working through could take place. In the last months of the analysis she had dreams of walking with the analyst sometimes arm in arm, sometimes hand in hand, and sometimes side by side. She was both furious and grateful that her analyst was actually letting her leave to have her own life and to have wishes that did not have to be realised. The dramatic enactment, a concrete thing that happened, led to the identification and labelling of a symbol, "the hug" that was now both enacted and known by analyst and analysand. Once "the hug" became a metaphor, the analysis could discover both the trauma and the ways it had become instinctualised in terms of wishes, fears, and defensive functions.

Discussion

The authors report two cases where an element of concreteness existing in the psychic life of each patient was due to the impact of trauma and gave rise to the tendency for enactments. Once the enactments were identified in a transference and countertransference context they gained symbolic meaning. Mr T was terrified that togetherness, even through the exchange of verbal communications, would lead to anni-hilation. He disavowed the multiple meanings of language and used language to create a deadened object relationship. As he expressed his desire for a tape recording of sessions and the analyst reflected on her concrete responses, his use of language to deaden became known. Now available for understanding was the way his character was structured to avoid contact. Ms M and her analyst created "the hug" before the summer vacation separation, awakening affects and fantasies in the dyad. The patient's collapse at the door and the analyst's response to go to her, to use her own body to balance the patient and then walk her to the couch was a clear interaction event. The enactment gained a name, "the hug", and became a symbol that led to the understanding of the patient's traumas and their sequelae. In reaction to the "hug" the analyst experienced feelings of comfort, transgression, damage, guilt, and shame as the patient expressed new belief in togetherness and love. Together they followed the associative path of physical contact and lack of contact to discover past seductions, abandonments, and the death of the baby she had never held. In both cases a symbolising process developed from the enactments. Here, the unconscious motivations to do to the analyst what had been done to them could be uncovered and followed back to a greater knowing of the original traumas.

In *Remembering, Repeating, and Working Through* (1914g), Freud wrote: "The patient does not remember anything of what he has forgotten and repressed, but acts it out. He reproduces it not as a memory but as an action" (p. 150). It is important to recognise that there are places in the mind that have never been symbolised due to overwhelming trauma. Terror enters the psyche and then appears in an enactment process sometimes in a continuous flow: Mr T's use of language to negate contact; and sometimes in a dramatic interaction: Ms M's collapse and the analyst's response. Stern (1983) elaborated on "unformulated material" … "that has literally never been thought" (p. 84). The two cases presented illustrate how experience of psychic trauma leaves a residue of concreteness that then presents in analytic treatment through action—in the form of a re-creation. Loewald (1980) wrote of "global transferences" characterising the "enactive form of remembering" where there is a substitution of the "… timelessness and lack of differentiation of the unconscious and of the primary process …" (p. 165). In the cases discussed here, the form of the "global transference" became apparent when the analyst reflected on countertransference reactions. The analysts in both cases were drawn into an action by becoming concrete in the interpretive process and physically responsive to distress. The terror of knowing the trauma resided also in the analyst's mind and remained unavailable until the enactments were recognised. Subsequently, attention to the action sequences and to the patient's compulsion to repeat allowed for fantasy constellations, reconstructions, and constructions of the unsymbolised. Enactments bring affect-laden fantasies into transference/countertransference. While action sequences accompany the narrative in psychoanalysis, this paper shows that where trauma has been significantly formative, the identification and analysis of concrete action sequences engender the symbolising and working through process. Under the press of affects, a mode of concreteness can be established in psychic functioning and pushes for an unfolding of enactment through which the traumatic affect and associated fantasies and events become known and explored. Even language, typically a symbolised function, can be an action annihilating its customary symbolic characteristic. Both patients held in their psyches a traumatising object relationship and neither had developed a narrative that could allow for a relating to their past and their present. As the analysands' inner worlds became less concrete and more knowable, the traumas and their defensive organisations in character and compromise formations entered a transformative process. In the beginning, the terror of trauma and the instinctual play of these traumatic scenes in the analysands' minds could only appear through enactment. The analytic dialogue served to unravel the unsymbolised action sequences that had worked their way into psychic systems of defence and adaptation, thereby allowing for the emergence of verbal symbolising narratives. As the symbolising process developed, reflection and working through in the transference and countertransference became possible.

References

Bass, A. (1997). The problem of concreteness. *Psychoanalytic Quarterly*, 66: 642–682.

Chused, J. (1991). The evocative power of enactments. *Journal of the American Psychoanalytic Association*, 3: 615–640.

Ellman, P. (1998). Is enactment a useful concept? In: S. Ellman & M. Moskowitz (Eds.), *Enactment: Toward a New Approach to the Therapeutic Relationship* (pp. 149–156). Northvale, NJ: Jason Aronson.

Ellman, S. J. & Moskowitz, M. (1998). *Enactment: Toward a New Approach in the Therapeutic Relationship*. Northvale, NJ: Jason Aronson.

Freedman, N., Barroso, F., Bucci, W. & Grand, S. (1978). The bodily manifestations of listening. *Psychoanalysis and Contemporary Thought, 1*: 157–164.

Freud, S. (1914g). *Remembering, Repeating and Working Through. S. E., 12.* London: Hogarth.

Goodman, N. (1998). The fixity of action in character enactments: Finding a developmental regression. In: S. Ellman & M. Moskowitz (Eds.), *Enactment: Toward a New Approach to the Therapeutic Relationship* (pp. 169–182). Northvale, NJ: Jason Aronson.

Goodman, N., Basseches, H., Ellman, P., Elmendorf, S., Fritsch, E., Helm, F. & Rockwell, S. (1993). The psychoanalytic mind at work: a study group investigation of listening (panel at IPA Congress, Amsterdam).

Jacobs, T. (1986). On countertransference enactment. *Journal of the American Psychoanalytic Association, 34*: 289–308.

Johan, M. (1992). Panel report: enactments in psychoanalysis. *Journal of the American Psychoanalytic Association, 40*: 827–841.

Katz, G. (1998). Where the action is. *Journal of the American Psychoanalytic Association, 46*: 1129–1168.

Kogan, I. (2007). *The Struggle against Mourning*. New York: Jason Aronson.

Laub, D. (1992). Bearing witness or the vicissitudes of listening. In: *Testimony: Crisis of Witnessing in Literature, Psychoanalysis, and History*. D. Laub & S. Felman (Eds.). New York: Routledge.

Lear, J. (2000). *Happiness, Death and the Remainder of Life*. Cambridge, MS: Harvard University Press.

Loewald, H. (1975). Psychoanalysis as an art and the fantasy character of the psychoanalytic situation. *Journal of the American Psychoanalytic Association, 23*: 277–299.

Loewald, H. (1980). *Papers on Psychoanalysis*. New Haven, CT: Yale University Press.

Loewald, H. (1986). Transference–countertransference. *Journal of the American Psychoanalytic Association, 34*: 275–287.

Reich, A. (1954). Early identifications as archaic elements in the superego. *Journal of the American Psychoanalytic Association, 2*: 218.

Sandler, J. (1960). On the concept of superego. *Psychoanalytic Study of the Child, 15*: 128–162.

Sandler, J. (1976). Countertransference and role-responsiveness. *International Review of Psychoanalysis, 3*: 43–47.

Segal, H. (1957). Notes on symbol formation. *International Journal of Psychoanalysis, 38*: 391–397.

Stern, D. B. (1983). Unformulated experience—from familiar chaos to creative disorder. *Contemporary Psychoanalysis, 19*: 71–99.

Tyson, R. & Renik, O. (1986). Countertransference in theory and practice. *Journal of the American Psychoanalytic Association, 34*: 699–708.

CHAPTER FIVE

The bureaucratisation of thought and language in groups and organisations

Laurence J. Gould

The map is not the territory

(anonymous)

We must understand that there can be no reconciliation without remembrance

(von Weizsäcker, 1985)

Introduction

The idea of concrete vs. abstract (symbolic, metaphoric) thinking is well-known and documented, both clinically in connection with schizophrenia (e.g., Searles, 1962), and developmentally with regard to cognitive growth (e.g., Piaget's (1985) groundbreaking work on concrete and formal operations). However, what is considerably less understood are both the "thinking style" of groups and organisations, as distinct from that of the individuals, within the normal range, who comprise them.

Early background

From its earliest days psychoanalysis has been interested in the nature of group and organisational processes. For example, in *Group Psychology and the Analysis of the Ego* (1921), Freud linked certain dynamic aspects of the Church and Army to his earlier hypotheses regarding the origins of social process and social structure—namely, in his analysis of the primal horde (1912–1913). Indeed, in his very first sentence in the 1921 paper he says: "The contrast between individual and social or group psychology, which at first glance may seem to be full of significance, loses a great deal of its sharpness when it is examined more closely" (p. 69). Fenichel (1946) later noted that human beings create social institutions to satisfy their needs as well as to accomplish required tasks, but that institutions then become external realities, comparatively independent of individuals that affect them in significant ways. However, despite this early interest in group psychology, and some sporadic, modest additions to a theory of group and institutional life, in for example, Freud's later "sociological works" (1927, 1930, 1939), neither he nor his colleagues carried this line of theorising much further. While the reasons are many, the paucity of psychoanalytic writings on the subject, especially early on, may partially attest to the conceptual limitations of a predominantly intrapsychic model of drive, and impulse/defence analysis for understanding any but a few selective aspects of group behaviour. The beginnings of an enlarged psychodynamic theory of group and organisational processes had to wait for a more fully worked out object relational perspective, which could provide the necessary interactive constructs.

Further developments

A radical and widely influential departure in group theory was not to happen until the publication of *Experiences in Groups* (1959) in which Bion put forward a psychoanalytic theory of group processes, based largely on developments in object relations theory pioneered by Melanie Klein (e.g., 1928, 1935, 1940, 1945, 1946, 1948, 1957) and her colleagues. The essential element of Bion's theory of group life was to differentiate between mental states, behaviours, and activities geared towards rational task performance, and those geared to emotional needs and anxieties. Following Klein, he viewed the latter as manifestations of experiences and unconscious phantasies originating in infancy. In addition to noting the importance of Klein's general theory of development centering on the paranoid/schizoid and depressive positions (see, Gould, 1997), Bion also explicitly set out to articulate the relevance of other central Kleinian concepts for understanding the human group, including: projective identification, splitting, psychotic anxiety, symbol formation, schizoid mechanisms, and part-objects. While there have been substantial advances since that time, Bion's work and the Kleinian concepts on which they are in part based, still remain the touchstones of psychoanalytic group theory. For the purposes of this chapter, however, it is only selected aspects of Bion's views regarding the nature of thinking and symbolisation, and their perturbations in groups and organisations, that are the focus.

Contrasting individual and group psychology

This is a familiar theme in social and political thought—the relationship between individual psychology and group psychology. In psychoanalysis proper, Freud (1921) elaborated some aspects of this issue, by pointing out, among others, how groups—in his examples, the Church and Army—developed particular cultures of thought and language that reflected underlying psychological processes. This chapter attempts to extend this notion, especially with reference to the work of Bion (1959), by placing it in the context of contemporary groups and organisations. The suggestion put forward is that over time, largely as a defence against the anxieties stimulated by increased complexity and rapid change, a particular, collective form of concrete thinking has developed, which is conceptualised here as "cognitive bureaucratisation". It is argued that many aspects of contemporary organisational life exemplify this process, from the development of cognitively debased thought patterns and forms of communication, to correlative schisms between groups, parties, and countries. Examples of these processes, and their negative consequences for group and organisational performance, and emotional well-being, at all levels, are explored.

A note on the confusion of levels

Before proceeding, I would like to note parenthetically that the process of cognitive transformations—in this instance the transformation of symbolic thought to concrete thinking in collectivities, presumably under the sway of regressive forces, like many psychoanalytic concepts, is often defined and used either somewhat differently, and/or in more restrictive versus inclusive ways. Further, Freud, for example, never specifically considered anything like the notion of such transforma- tions as an aspect of a collectivity responding to conflict, trauma, or loss, except by implication in *Group Psychology and the Analysis of the Ego* (1921), where his first line is, "The contrast between individual psychol- ogy and social or group psychology, which at first glance may seem to be full of significance, loses a great deal of its sharpness when it is exam- ined more closely." He also, picked up this theme, albeit again indi- rectly, in *Totem and Taboo* (1912–1913), with the totem being a particular kind of memorial, erected by the guilt-ridden sons in expiation for the murder of the primal father. I put forward these notions since I hope to suggest that linguistic transformations in collectivities, as a conse- quence of conflict, trauma, or loss, serve the same defensive functions as they do for individuals. However, it also seems clear that the concept of concrete thinking in connection with individuals does not capture either the processes or the manifestations of concretisation on a collec- tive level. I believe, therefore, that conceptualising concretisation with regard to collectivities, requires both a different level of analysis, as well as a different praxis, since the work of restoring symbolic function- ing takes place in forms and venues not at all like therapeutic work that takes place in the consulting room. For example, the conditions under which the processes of interpreting the defensive functions of concre- tisation in the treatment situation take place under relatively control- led conditions, with highly regulated boundaries. By contrast, none of these conditions is likely to prevail in response to societal conflicts and trauma that result in collective, regressive functioning. Added to this are, of course, the differences of working in treatment with one indi- vidual, with his or her unique history, compared to the complexities of working in groups, with the needs, and preferred defensive styles of the individuals comprising the group, highly varied.

From what I have stated up to this point, I think that you can begin to see where I am heading. It is an attempt to grapple conceptually, and with the enormous potential implications for understanding what hap- pens in groups cognitively, as well as applying a psychoanalytic under- standing to catastrophic, collective trauma and conflict, that groups, organisations, and society increasingly face. Parenthetically this form of applied psychoanalysis, pioneered at the Tavistock Institute, has a long, rich history, and in current usage is commonly referred to as socio-analysis, or systems psychodynamics (Gould, 2003). To make these terms explicit, perhaps the best short definition is offered by Bion (1959), who notes in his introduction to *Experiences in Groups* that:

> The term "group therapy" can have two meanings. It can refer to the treatment of a number of individuals ... or it can refer to ... an endeavour to develop in a group the forces that lead to ... cooperative activity. The therapy of groups [as distinct from group therapy (author's addition)] is likely to turn on the acquisition of knowledge and experience of the factors that make for good group spirit. (p. 10)

If we take this quote broadly, which I believe would clearly be in the spirit of Bion's thinking, the collective—whatever dilemmas, conflicts, and traumas it may be grappling with—becomes the object of enquiry and intervention. This constitutes the subject and praxis of socio-analysis.

Bion's conception of group psychology

Compared with Freud, as noted above in connection with the differences between individual and group psychology "losing their sharpness", Bion is quite explicit with regard to understanding group level phenomena, emphasising that they cannot be reduced to individual psychology. In this sense he departs quite markedly from Freud's view noted above. In fact, Bion is so scrupulous about making this point, that the language of his group theory is comprised almost exclusively of non-psychoanalytic neologisms, the most central being "basic assumptions".

Since Bion's basic assumption theory is well known, it will not be reviewed in detail. Suffice it to say, therefore, that the basic assumptions—fight/flight (baF), dependency (baD), and pairing (baP)—may be viewed as modes of group behaviour which coalesce around different patterns of drives, affects, mental contents, object relations, and defences. These basic assumptions are aspects of group behaviour in which the aim, as well as the source, relate to emotional security.

They are contrasted by Bion with another mode—namely, the work or "W" group—the aim of which is rational, reality-based, task performance. It is in this connection that I specifically begin to consider the question of language and cognition in groups and organisations, and how they may be understood as an expression of social (collective) defences, required to defend against anxiety.

Regressive behaviour and cognitively debased language

Alongside the work group, which functions in a way that draws on the "mature" capabilities of its members, "ba group" functioning may be considered a form of "groupthink",[1] characterised by a lack of critical awareness, non-differentiation, and magical thinking. In Bion's view, such states of mind and their manifest corollaries in thought, language, and behaviour can be viewed as defences against anxiety—with anxiety viewed as having its origins in the emotional demands and complex challenges the group must meet. It is in the face of these that the group retreats into the socio-emotional patterns of denial described by the bas. Further, in such groups an unconscious, collusive bond develops between the members that reinforces denial. The casualty of this process is work. For in such ba states, the group is given to stereotyping and simplifying external reality, and internally fostering a culture of undifferentiated, uncritical mutual support. In this later process, aside from the damage to required work, there is also collateral damage of another sort—namely, powerful pressures to relinquish individuality.

The fate of the dissenter in ba groups

In connection with the above, one may also consider the fate of a group member who questions the assumptive reality of the ba group. As Krantz (2006) points out, the result is often severe and decisive consequences. Differentiation within the fused, harmonised emotional environment of the basic assumption group is experienced as—and in a very real sense is—a betrayal. That is, the naysayer is viewed as a threat to the ba group's existence in a blissful state of denial, platitude, and dogma. And it is precisely such linguistic forms—the group's *lingua franca*—and their enforcement by the group (the marginalisation or expulsion of those with "foreign accents"), that function to maintain a "*ba* culture". In sum, a cognitive/linguistic system exhibiting all the hallmarks of a bureaucracy: severely diminished discretionary behaviour, inflexibility, and a literalist, "biblical" adherence to policies, rules, and regulations.

Cognitively debased language and verbal communication

To further elaborate the view outlined above, it is useful to specifically consider the nature of verbal communication in ba groups. As Bion views it, functional, constructive communication is a property of the work group. By contrast, the closer a group comes to operating on a *ba* level, the less it uses rational communication as a mode of discourse. Early on, Klein (1930) stressed the developmental importance of symbol formation, and the consequences of this capacity breaking down. Bion suggests that in ba groups, this is precisely what happens as well. That is, the ba group loses the capacity for symbolisation, and in its stead, as Bion suggests, the ba group uses existing language as a mode of action, concretising thought in a manner, for example, in which the group acts in relation to the "map" rather than the territory it symbolises. Bion (1959, pp. 186–187) provides a powerful example, citing the biblical account of the building of the Tower of Babel (Genesis xi. 1–9). He postulates that the symbolism of a tower, which would reach heaven, introduces the idea of Messianic hope. But as the group concretises the idea of salvation, and acts upon it by building the Tower, it brings down the wrath of Yahweh, who confuses their language, and scatters them throughout the earth. This parable if generalised and put into ordinary form, is a parable of a group destroyed by acting on a false (concrete) belief. Further, and quite central, is that the particular form of destruction is verbal fragmentation, with Babel a metaphor for the multiplication of self-contained, hermetic linguistic systems. But what I would like to emphasise here is that this idea can be framed succinctly as a hypothesis about language and communication in groups, as follows.

Groups in a state of mind, characterised by consensual, concrete thinking, and debased verbal communication, acting on the aims they suggest, result in a catastrophic failure of communication, and the demise of the group in fragmentation.

Put slightly differently, the point can be made that the obverse of groups in the thrall of basic assumption life, marked by cohesive and restrictive language, when acted upon, results (metaphorically) in the fragmentation of language, and the group's ultimate destruction.

That is, if a group is incapable of authentically communicating, internally or externally, neither redemption, nor even a return to the *status quo ante*, is possible.

Paranoid/schizoid and depressive positions

What I have just written about leaders and organisations driven by the enactment of unresolved depressive position processes, is the obverse of the more familiar forms of overt malignant leadership informed almost exclusively by perverse paranoid/schizoid states of mind—the Hitlers, Husseins, Milosovics of the world, with policies like the "final solution" and "ethnic cleansing" being the extreme of violent, sadistic, and destructive splitting. Or less malignantly, the Margaret Thatchers, Bibi Netanyahus, or Richard Nixons. In such cases it is easy, on the face of it, to literally see what it means to destroy the moral order because the "centre" is a centre in name only—it is comprised of a leadership cadre that perpetuates and stimulates anxiety and hatred rather than containing it, resulting in violence, dehumanisation, and destructiveness that others enact on its behalf. But I would like to emphasise that these leaders and their followers represent in important ways the converse of what I have described as the perversions of depressive position values—the psychically corrupted depressive position leader is married to the sadistic psychopathic paranoid/schizoid leader: they are a mutual creation.

References

Bion, W. R. (1959). *Experiences in Groups and Other Papers*. London: Tavistock (PEP version).

Fenichel, O. (1946). *The Psychoanalytic Theory of Neurosis*. London: Kegan Paul, Trench, Trubner.

Freud, S. (1912–1913). *Totem and Taboo. S. E., 13*. London: Hogarth.

Freud, S. (1921). *Group Psychology and the Analysis of the Ego. S. E., 18*. London: Hogarth.

Freud, S. (1927). *The Future of an Illusion. S. E., 21*. London: Hogarth.

Freud, S. (1930). *Civilization and Its Discontents. S. E., 21*. London: Hogarth.

Freud, S. (1939). *Moses and Monotheism. S. E., 23*. London: Hogarth.

Gould, L. J. (1997). Correspondences between Bion's basic assumption theory and Klein's developmental positions: An outline. *Free Associations*, 7: 15–30.

Gould, L. J. (2003). "Collective working through: The role and function of memorialization." Presented at: Memory, Memorials and Collective Working Through. Annual Meeting of the New York Freudian Society, co-sponsored by Pace University, Downtown NYC, Psychology Department. February 8.

Klein, M. (1928). Early stages of the Oedipus conflict. *International Journal of Psychoanalysis*, 9: 167–180.

Klein, M. (1935). A contribution to the psychogenesis of manic-depressive states. *International Journal of Psychoanalysis*, 16: 145–174.

Klein, M. (1940). Mourning and its relation to manic-depressive states. *International Journal of Psychoanalysis*, 21: 125–153.

Klein, M. (1945). The Oedipus complex in the light of early anxieties. *International Journal of Psychoanalysis*, 26: 11–33.

Klein, M. (1946). Notes on some schizoid mechanisms. *International Journal of Psychoanalysis*, 27: 99–110.

Klein, M. (1948). A contribution to the theory of anxiety and guilt. *International Journal of Psychoanalysis*, 29: 114–123.

Klein, M. (1957). Envy and gratitude. In: *Envy and Gratitude and Other Works*, 1946–1963 (pp. 176–234). New York: Free Press.

Krantz, J. (2006). Leadership, betrayal and adaptation. *Human Relations*, 59(2): 221–240.

Piaget, J. (1985). *The Equilibration of Cognitive Structures: The Central Problem of Intellectual Development*. Chicago: University of Chicago Press.

Searles, H. F. (1962). The differentiation between concrete and metaphorical thinking in the recovering schizophrenic patient. *Journal of the American Psychoanalytic Association*, 10(1): 22–49.

Whyte, W. H. Jr. (1952). Groupthink. *Fortune*, March.

Note

1. *Groupthink* was the title of an article in Fortune magazine in March 1952 by William H. Whyte Jr. He wrote:

> Groupthink is becoming a national philosophy. Groupthink being a coinage—and, admittedly, a loaded one—a working definition is in order. We are not talking about mere instinctive conformity—it is, after all, a perennial failing of mankind. What we are talking about is a rationalized conformity—an open, articulate philosophy which holds that group values are not only expedient but right and good as well.

Whyte derided the notion he argued was held by a trained elite of Washington's social engineers.

Groupthink is a type of thought exhibited by group members who try to minimise conflict and reach consensus without critically testing, analysing, and evaluating ideas. Individual creativity, uniqueness, and independent thinking are lost in the pursuit of group cohesiveness, as are the advantages of reasonable balance in choice and thought that might normally be obtained by making decisions as a group. During groupthink, members of the group avoid promoting viewpoints outside the comfort zone of consensus thinking. A variety of motives for this may exist, such as a desire to avoid being seen as foolish, or a desire to avoid embarrassing or angering other members of the group. Groupthink may cause groups to make hasty, irrational decisions, where individual doubts are set aside, for fear of upsetting the group's balance. The term is frequently used pejoratively, with hindsight.

CHAPTER SIX

Painting poppies: on the relationship between concrete and metaphorical thinking

Caron E. Harrang

Introduction

Wilfred Bion (1965) begins his book on *Transformations* thus:

> Suppose a painter sees a path through a field sown with poppies
> and paints it: at one end of the chain of events is the field of pop-
> pies, at the other a canvas with pigment disposed on its surface.
> We can recognize that the latter represents the former, so I shall
> suppose that despite the differences between a field of poppies
> and a piece of canvas, despite the transformation that the artist
> has effected in what he saw to make it take the form of a picture,
> *something* has remained unaltered and on this *something* recognition
> depends. (p. 1)

In this deceptively simple description Bion shows us the relationship
between concrete reality and any symbolic rendering of that reality.
He uses this analogy to demonstrate how the analyst's experience of
the patient's production of unconscious thoughts and feelings is transformed into psychoanalytic interpretations. I will use it in a slightly
different way to shed light on the relationship between concrete and

metaphorical thinking and show how it relates to Melanie Klein's theory of mental positions (1935, 1946) as elaborated by Bion (1963) and later by Ronald Britton (1998). Concreteness as it is usually defined in the psychoanalytic literature to describe a pathological condition is amended in favour of a view that it is also a natural component of the paranoid-schizoid position, just as metaphorical or symbolic thinking is a natural component of the depressive position. As such, concrete thinking is not overcome or outgrown as the individual develops the capacity for metaphorical thinking. More accurately, I believe, in health it is balanced with metaphorical thinking in a way that allows for ongoing, unconscious oscillations between these two forms of thought necessary for mental growth.

Furthermore, I concur with Britton (1998) who believes that there are pathological and healthy forms of both the paranoid-schizoid and the depressive position. Applying his model I suggest that it is possible to observe instances of concrete thinking in the clinical situation that are non-pathological and, as such, part of the normal paranoid-schizoid position in which there is a transitory return to sensory-based perceptual experience that is pre-symbolic. I will provide clinical material and ordinary non-analytic conversation to illustrate these phenomena and show how concreteness may either be part of healthy development or indicate what Harold Searles (1962) calls "pseudo-concreteness", where ego boundaries are actively obscured and the individual's thoughts and feelings remain undifferentiated, neither genuinely concrete nor clearly symbolic. I will also contrast non-pathological concreteness with what Bass (1997), Frosch (1995), Grossman (1996), Jacobson (1957), and Renik (1992) describe as an attitude of absolute certainty about one's perceptions that rigidly defends against the possibility that "one thing might mean another" (Bass, p. 645). Implications of the views expressed in this chapter for psychoanalytic technique are briefly mentioned.

Background

Before proceeding to examine the relationship between concrete and metaphorical thinking as it relates to Klein's mental positions, it is necessary to touch on terminology. Concreteness in common linguistic usage refers to things perceived as real, because they can be seen or touched as contrasted with, for example, thoughts or feelings that do not exist in physical form. Developmental psychologists such as Piaget (1945, 1954) describe concrete thinking as a phase of cognitive development that precedes the capacity for abstract or metaphorical thinking characterised by literalness and lack of generalisation. Psychoanalysts, on the other hand, have tended to focus on the unconscious, dynamic roots of concrete thinking, linking it generally to difficulties in differentiating concrete from symbolic communication. Hanna Segal (1957, p. 391) illustrates this problem in her well-known paper, *Notes on Symbol Formation*, when she describes a schizophrenic man's inability to play his violin because it has become for him indistinguishable from masturbating in public. Harold Searles (1959, p. 305) notes something similar in his work with schizophrenic patients, saying, "If his therapist uses symbolic language, he may experience this in literal terms; and on the other hand the affairs of daily life (eating, dressing, sleeping and so on) which we think of as literal and concrete, he may react to as possessing a unique symbolic significance which completely obscures their 'practical' importance in his life as a human being." Alan Bass (1997, pp. 643–644) describes another form of concreteness evident in non-psychotic, narcissistically organised individuals who are so utterly convinced of the truth of their own perceptions that they are unable to consider the analyst's point of view when it differs from their own. For example, the patient may begin the session refusing to talk because she *knows* that the analyst will be disapproving or critical. Dramatic as these descriptions are they serve well to illustrate the essence of concrete thinking in its pathological forms. Non-pathological concrete thinking associated with the normal paranoid-schizoid position will be described later in this chapter.

A metaphor is a figure of speech concisely expressed by comparing two things, saying that one is the other, as for example, in Bion suggesting that the artist's painting is the analyst's interpretation. Metaphors are not meaningful, however, unless the difference between the two things being compared is also understood. The schizophrenic man Segal described could not differentiate playing a musical instrument in public from a private sexual act. Thus, playing the violin was not in any way metaphorical because the two things being compared were experienced by him as identical. In his introduction to *Attention and Interpretation* Bion (1970) notes that what gives analogy [and perhaps all metaphor] its communicative power is the *relationship* between the things being compared and not the things themselves. From a psychoanalytic perspective, metaphorical or symbolic thinking (these terms are used interchangeably) implies the capacity for differentiation between self and object. How this mental ability develops is viewed differently by various psychoanalytic schools. For example, Klein (1930) viewed symbol formation—and by extension metaphorical thinking—as resulting from the ego's efforts to deal with anxieties evoked by its relationship to internal and external objects.

To summarise, terms such as "concreteness" or "concrete thinking" have generally been used in the psychoanalytic literature to denote a developmental stage preceding the capacity for symbolisation and metaphorical thinking, or to describe a state of mind that accompanies regression and defends against differentiation and mental growth. Segal (1957) linked the symbolising process with achievement of the depressive position. Conversely, she believed that "disturbances in differentiation between ego and object lead to disturbances in differentiation between the symbol and the object symbolized and therefore to *concrete thinking characteristic of psychoses* [my emphasis]" (p. 393). In other words, concreteness or concrete thinking is used as an antonym to symbolisation or metaphorical thinking. This view of the relationship between concrete and metaphorical thinking is reflected in the writings of Kleinian and non-Kleinian analysts alike. Although I agree that this terminology does accurately describe an important aspect of mental life, it ignores or does not account for another dimension of the relationship between concrete and metaphorical thinking that is complementary. In the next section I will show how Kleinian metapsychology as elaborated by Bion and Britton helps to illuminate the non-pathological relationship between concrete and metaphorical thinking.

An evolving understanding of the paranoid-schizoid and depressive positions

Klein elaborated and greatly animated Freud's concept of the ego through her introduction of the depressive position (1935) and later the paranoid-schizoid position (1946). Together they form the core of Kleinian metapsychology. The paranoid-schizoid position is characterised by part-object representations of the infant's experience of its relationships with primary objects.[1] Self and object are initially experienced as exaggeratedly "good" or "bad" with the aim of union with gratifying, good objects and expulsion of frustrating, bad objects. The experience of separation between self and object in the first months of the infant's life is relatively undeveloped mentally such that distinctions between internal and external, or hallucinatory wish-fulfilment versus actual gratification are only vaguely recognised. A primary defence against psychotic anxieties, such as the fear of being poisoned or devoured (Klein, 1946, p. 2), is projective identification[2] in which unwanted parts of the self are unconsciously attributed to the object. Similarly, qualities of the external environment including the parents and others are introjected and treated as part of the self. Through an ongoing process of projection and introjection part-objects are transformed into whole objects where "good" and "bad" experiences are gradually integrated.

According to Klein (1935, 1946) the depressive position forms because of the infant's capacity to differentiate self and object, thus allowing for integration of libidinal and destructive impulses and furthering the development of psychic reality. The ability to feel love and hate for the same object, no longer split into excessively "good" and "bad" part-objects, allows the infant to feel "states akin to mourning ... because aggressive impulses are felt to be directed against the loved object" (1946, p. 14). This newly forming capacity to feel emotional pain over phantasised destructiveness towards whole objects combined with the impulse towards reparation fuels emotional growth. For example, a six-month-old infant furious at mother for frustrating his desire to be picked up and comforted may offer to share a favourite toy or a bite of the half-eaten biscuit she gave him after feeling his needs adequately recognised. Gestures like these signal the developing child's ability through symbolic means to demonstrate concern for the effect of his thoughts, feelings, and actions on the object. Thus, as Segal (1957) emphasised, achievement of the infantile depressive position is intimately linked with symbol formation and the beginning of metaphorical thinking.

Klein (1946) viewed the paranoid-schizoid position as preceding the depressive position which will then consolidate in the first few years of the child's life. If persecutory fears associated with the paranoid-schizoid position are not adequately resolved, they may interfere with development of the depressive position, going on to form the basis of later manic-depressive and schizophrenic illnesses. Once it is reliably achieved, movement from the depressive position back to the paranoid-schizoid was *primarily* seen as pathological. However, as Britton (1998, p. 70) notes, a close examination of Klein's writings shows that "She described the paranoid-schizoid position sometimes as a defense, sometimes as a regression and sometimes as part of [normal] development." This variability in Klein's terminology may be one reason why her highly original contribution is sometimes misunderstood to refer exclusively to the initial formation of the paranoid-schizoid and depressive positions as if they were solely developmental stages. Fortunately, two of Klein's followers, Wilfred Bion and Ronald Britton, have made important revisions to her theory of the positions in ways that, I believe, strengthen its viability, and provide a platform for my own thoughts on the relationship between concrete and metaphorical thinking detailed in this chapter.

In *Elements* (1963, p. 3), Bion advanced the notion that Klein's paranoid-schizoid (Ps) and depressive positions (D) could be thought of as proceeding from one to the other *in either direction*, which he represented in the equation Ps↔D. In placing the double arrow between the two positions he inferred from Klein's writings that movement back and forth between the positions was *at times* part of development. This he restated as a naturally occurring oscillation throughout the lifespan. Bion left intact Klein's descriptions of the positions, adding that it was possible to experience "a state of mind analogous to the paranoid-schizoid position" (1970, p. 124), characterised by unknowing, frustration, and suffering as one waits, without memory or desire, for meaning to evolve. He realised that the paranoid-schizoid position was not only a pathological state as Klein had described but a source of immense creativity as well—if the individual could bear what Keats (1817) called "negative capability", or openness to "uncertainties, Mysteries, [and] doubts without any irritable reaching after fact & reason". He saw this non-pathological paranoid-schizoid position as a necessary precondition for, among other things, analytic listening and optimal receptivity to the patient's emotional experience. Unfortunately, rather than calling his expansion the normal paranoid-schizoid position, he coined the term "patience" to distinguish it from the pathological state. However, as Britton (1998, p. 69) notes, it was never accepted as a psychoanalytic term.

Building on Bion's revision of Klein's theory, Britton (1998) wrote a theoretical paper entitled *Before and After the Depressive Position* in which he sought to clarify how movement between the positions reflects either psychic development or regression. His model clearly distinguishes between the pathological paranoid-schizoid position described by Klein and the normal paranoid-schizoid position that Bion called "patience". Additionally, Britton (p. 72) identifies a pathological form of the depressive position, not explicitly recognised by Klein or Bion, and characterised by a "ready-made, previously espoused coherent belief system … prompted by a wish to end uncertainty and the fears associated with fragmentation". For example, the certainty with which the Bush administration sought (erroneously) to connect the attacks on 9/11 with the then Iraqi dictator, Saddam Hussein, typifies the moralistic and self-righteous character of the pseudo-depressive position. This state of mind results, Britton says, from an inability to surrender the security, moral sensibility, and self-reflective capacity of the normal depressive position in order to re-enter the more anxiety-laden territory of the normal paranoid-schizoid position necessary for emotional growth. Psychic development occurs when there is uninterrupted movement from the normal paranoid-schizoid position into the depressive position followed by a return to the next paranoid-schizoid position … and so on. This clarification of Bion's formula underscores the normalcy of the paranoid-schizoid position, indeed, the importance of it for ongoing emotional growth. Regression,[3] on the other hand, refers to a shift into either the pathological paranoid-schizoid position or the pathological depressive position.

Concrete and metaphorical thinking—a post-Kleinian view

Holding in mind Klein's theory of the positions as elaborated by Bion and Britton, the question remains: what does this tell us about concrete and metaphorical thinking? Returning to the central thesis of this chapter I suggest that there are both healthy and pathological forms of concrete thinking, and that oscillation between concrete and metaphorical thinking are part of an ordinary, non-pathological process of development. My conceptualisation runs parallel to Britton's model; that is, mental growth results from ongoing shifts back and forth between part-object and whole object relating. Non-pathological concreteness is, in my view, a natural component of the normal paranoid-schizoid position. This view implies that concrete thinking is pathological only when it becomes fixed and impedes movement between the positions. Concreteness as an obstacle to growth is seen as belonging to either the pathological paranoid-schizoid or pathological depressive position.

Logically it follows that there are also healthy and pathological forms of metaphorical thinking. For example, applying the often quoted phrase "God helps those who help themselves" (Sidney, 1698, cited in Keyes, 2006, p. 79) to mean that it is ungodly or morally wrong to depend on others illustrates pathological metaphorical thinking. Genuine metaphorical thinking as previously mentioned (Segal, 1957) belongs to the depressive position, whereas errors in symbolisation, such as the "unique symbolic significance" (Searles, 1959, p. 305) which schizophrenic individuals assign to ordinary concrete acts such as eating or sleeping, may be thought of as belonging to the pathological paranoid-schizoid position. However, it is beyond the scope of this chapter to explore in any depth the pathological forms of metaphorical thinking. Rather, I will elaborate what I mean by non-pathological concreteness, as compared with its pathological forms, and show how this relates to the paranoid-schizoid position. As stated earlier, this healthy form of concreteness is, I believe, complementary to the development of metaphorical thinking and not its opposite, as is often implied in the literature.

Concrete thinking in the paranoid-schizoid position

The essence of non-pathological concrete thinking is, in my view, to be found in sensate experience. It is, for example, represented in the infant's visual experience of gazing at the mother's face before he has any conceptual understanding of what he is seeing. It is the feel of her skin against his as she attends to his physical needs for feeding, bathing, nappy changing, and dressing before he has a clearly formed sense of the physical or emotional boundaries between himself and her. It is the taste of warm milk entering his mouth as he suckles, and the sensations associated with swallowing and digestion before he understands that what he is doing is called nursing. It is hearing the sound of his own voice as he cries—expressing a multiplicity of primitive anxieties—and how this proto-mental experience changes as he registers the vibrations of mother's approaching footsteps and then her voice as she speaks before taking him into her arms. Altogether these body-based, somatopsychic experiences form the substrate of what, in normal circumstances, gradually becomes symbolised in verbal thoughts and speech.

This way of understanding the relationship between concrete and symbolic or metaphorical thinking may have been what Ernest Jones (1916, cited in Segal, 1957, p. 392) had in mind when he said that all symbols represent experiences of "the self and of immediate blood relations and of the phenomena of birth, life, and death".

Put another way, it seems to me unlikely that there is any such thing as a symbol that is *not* rooted, however distantly or unconsciously, in sensory experience. This, I believe, is what Bion was referencing when he noted that any symbolically expressed creative impulse, be it the artist's painting or the analyst's interpretation, draws upon "what he saw"—that is, a sensory experience—which allows recognition of the relationship between the symbol and what is symbolised. Along similar lines, Searles (1962, p. 582) notes "the extent to which somatic sensations participate in the development of metaphorical thinking in the normal child". That is, "Before the child can come to understand such phrases as 'gives me a pain in the neck', or 'turns my stomach', or 'tears at my heartstrings' in their metaphorical meaning, relatively devoid of somatic concomitants, he must first have *felt* their meaning as a partially, or perhaps predominately, somatic experience." I agree with this if by "devoid of somatic concomitants" it is to be understood that metaphorical meaning contains the literal level of experience rather than replacing it.

The significance of sensory experience to metaphorical thinking was also noted by the writer T. S. Eliot (1919, cited in 1950, pp. 124–125), when he posited the "objective correlative"[4] or "a set of objects, a situation, a chain of events which shall be the formula of that particular emotion; such that when the external facts, *which must terminate in sensory experience*, are given, the emotion is immediately evoked [my emphasis]". This concept reflected his conviction that human emotional experience is dependent on the ability to locate objects in the external world which reflect the living power of our thoughts. Eliot was quick to point out that it is not the object or image in isolation that evokes an emotional response. Rather, feeling originates in response to the combination of these phenomena as they appear together.

The relationship between non-pathological concrete and metaphorical thinking may also be reflected in Freud's (1896) ideas about the origins of consciousness and the relationship between what he called "thing-presentation" and "word-presentation". Thing-presentation is a visual image in the unconscious unconnected to a linguistic signifier. Word-presentation is a conscious thought comprised of "the presentation of the thing, plus the presentation of the word belonging to it ..." (1915e, p. 201). He believed that conscious thought arose when thing-presentations become linked with language. Freud's belief that both thing-presentation and word-presentation are derived from "sense-perceptions" (p. 202) is significant for my definition of non-pathological concrete thinking. If we accept that thing-presentation corresponds to concrete thinking and word-presentation to metaphorical thinking, then Freud is saying that both forms of mental activity are rooted in sensory experience. Thus, we can conclude that sensory experiences meld with thing-presentations and gradually acquire lexical meaning in normal development.

The paranoid-schizoid position from infancy on is, in my view, embedded in sensory-based perceptual experience. These sensory experiences are represented concretely before they acquire full symbolic value. Development hinges, of course, on the depressive position having been relatively well established in the first few years of life. That is, the infantile depressive position is the prerequisite without which the normal paranoid-schizoid position would be impossible. Once achieved, the post-depressive paranoid-schizoid position bears the initial impact of new thoughts and feelings. The capacity to think in literal imagistic terms relatively unencumbered by reality testing accompanies the necessary deconstruction of meaning found in previously achieved depressive positions. If the disorganisation, lack of coherence, and uncertainty associated with the normal paranoid-schizoid position can be tolerated and contained, then a new experience, at first represented literally, acquires symbolic value as the next depressive position takes shape.

As previously noted, by Segal and Searles among others, concrete thinking may become distorted and part of disordered thinking evident in schizophrenia and borderline disorders. Before turning to illustrations of non-pathological concreteness in the next section it is important to note the distinguishing features of its pathological forms. Concreteness accompanying psychosis obscures developing metaphorical meaning or strips it away in a process Searles (1962, p. 580) termed "desymbolization" where "once-*attained* metaphorical meanings" are reacted to as literal or concrete. This denuding of symbolic significance is one indication of a defence against the self-object differentiation necessary for movement into the depressive position. Active destruction of metaphorical meaning for the purpose of evading growth is, in my view, part of the pathological paranoid-schizoid position. By contrast, concrete thinking in non-psychotic, narcissistically organised individuals evidenced by the conviction that their point of view is the absolute truth, described by Bass and others, is more likely indicative of the pathological depressive position. Concreteness in this state of mind is used to defend against the perceived crisis of relinquishing the depressive position and experiencing, once again, the emotional turbulence and lack of certainty associated with the normal paranoid-schizoid position.

Illustrations of non-pathological concrete thinking

An ordinary (non-clinical) example

The first example of non-pathological concrete thinking comes from an ordinary, non-clinical conversation with actor Sidney Poitier in an interview he gave to Renee Montagne, host of *Morning Edition*, and aired on NPR (national public radio in the United States (May 19–20, 2009). Poitier, now in his eighties, was describing his childhood in the remote village of Arthur's Town on Cat Island in the Bahamas where his family lived without access to electricity, indoor plumbing, or motorised transportation for the first ten years of his life. The interviewer asked how under such circumstances he became interested in acting. Poitier explained that around the age of ten his family moved from Cat Island to Nassau where he was for the first time introduced to the world of modern conveniences. One day a group of boyhood friends asked if he wanted to join them in attending a matinee. Having no idea what a matinee was, and perhaps too shy to reveal his ignorance, yet curious, he agreed to go with them. Although he no longer recalls the title of the film, he remembers that it was a Hollywood Western. Transfixed by images of cowboys walking, talking, and riding around in horse-drawn carriages, he wondered "How could they get all those people in this little place, this little theater place ...?"

Afterwards as Poitier and his pals were walking home he was overcome with an irresistible urge to return to the theatre and learn about this thing called a matinee that had so "shocked" his young imagination. Laughingly, he told Montagne that he stood at the back door of the theatre "waiting to see who would come out", not understanding that what he had seen was on the screen and not in the theatre as he had experienced it. That is, the overwhelming power of the visual and emotional experience was such that he did not initially recognise the distinction between internal and external reality. This transient lack of differentiation between inner and outer, combined with an intensely felt sensorial experience, in my view characterises non-pathological concreteness in normal individuals. In a less healthy individual this might have become the basis of a delusion; that is, an enduring conviction that the film characters were real in the external sense, indistinguishable from a representation of that reality in film or in one's imagination. Or someone less curious might simply have dismissed his unknowing as not worth pursuing. As it was, the emotional intensity of the above-mentioned experience, initially felt as literal and concrete, was eventually transformed into Poitier's meaningful, reality-oriented, professional career. How this transformation came about is also significant for understanding the nature of normal concrete thinking and how it relates to the shift from the paranoid-schizoid to the depressive position.

Poitier (2008, pp. 4–5) describes how his first film experience was transformed from a literal event into one that served as inspiration for his eventual career as an actor through an interaction with one of his siblings. His older sister, Teddy, asked him, after he had seen the film, what he wanted to be when he grew up. Poitier spontaneously announced that he wanted to go to Hollywood so that he could "work with cows". It was then, he speculates, that she must have figured "that since it was in the movies that I had seen cows, I must have assumed that in order to be one of the heroic cowboys from the movies, I had to go to Hollywood". When his sister sensitively explained that Hollywood was a place where they made movies and not where one went to literally become a cowboy, the would-be actor felt severely "disappointed" and concluded that his "future was to lie elsewhere".

Although the preceding vignette is not from an analytic treatment, we can see that the sister functions much as a good analyst does by careful listening and respectfully interpreting her brother's phantasy. Poitier's disappointment indicates his recognition of the sister's clarifying understanding helping him move from an idealised phantasy (paranoid-schizoid position) to a more realistic appraisal (depressive position) of the opportunities that lay ahead in Hollywood. These opportunities included, ironically, his starring in two Westerns and later becoming the first African American actor to win an academy award (1963) for his role in *Lilies of the Field*.

In considering this vignette, which by necessity omits important details of the actor's life, I am, nonetheless, left with the impression that the concrete nature of his experience—thinking that the people and animals were three-dimensionally present in the theatre—contributed to his development as an actor and richly creative human being. With the help of Poitier's sister, he could distinguish between what was on the screen and what was in his mind, and thus could bear the loss of his concrete phantasy, identifying with the actors as whole objects separate from himself.

Clinical examples

A second example of non-pathological concrete thinking comes from the written report of an analytic candidate (Parnes, 2009), looking back on his year-long experience of infant observation. Although the experience is described retrospectively using metaphorical language—that is, from the depressive position—it conveys both the candidate's conjecture of the infant's sensory-based perceptual mode of thinking and his own ability to surrender to an analogous state of mind:

> At first, like [the infant], I am awash in sensory experience. I notice the mountain views, the feel of the home (quiet and orderly), the sun coming through the window, the temperature of the bathwater. And I can't leave out the breast, which I take in with my eyes as [the infant] does with his mouth. He is tongue tied[5] and so am I. It is all so much to take in and neither of us knows what it all means.

The candidate's capacity to relinquish the depressive position and feel "awash in sensory experience", where "it is all so much to take in" allows him to get closer to the infant's experience, and learn about psychic development in an emotionally meaningful way. This ability to temporarily forego knowing "what it all means" is as much a part of psychic growth and development for the observer as it is for the infant.

A third and final example of non-pathological concrete thinking comes from my analysis of a married middle-aged professional man with a predominately obsessive character structure and strong tendencies to somatisation. At the time of the following vignette, the patient felt emboldened to express his increasingly conscious ambivalence towards analysis and the analyst with less trepidation than in the past, although this often resulted in a flare-up of somatic symptoms, particularly during weekend breaks and vacations.

The patient began the session talking about a friend's behaviour disordered child who hates being touched and has "learning difficulties" at school. Further exploration of this material led to my patient's speculation that the child acts up at school when he feels ignored by the teacher. Then he thought of three missed sessions in a previous week and wondered if I would allow him to reschedule since "nothing had happened" during these hours. In exploring his feelings about the missed sessions, it became possible to show him how he felt extremely persecuted by the unconscious perception that he was a "no-thing" (did not exist) in the analyst's mind during these times. This had caused him to feel both untouched and untouchable, which he reversed in the association to the neighbour's son who "hates being touched". Unconsciously, he also blamed the analyst particularly for his hateful feelings, which added to his fears of being retaliated against. As his feelings associated with these events were taken up, one by one in the session, the patient gradually experienced a sense of relief and then, quite unexpectedly, strong loving feelings arose. Spontaneously he confided, "After you said what you just said I heard myself say in my mind, 'I love you!'." This was said in a tone of voice conveying that he felt both appalled and in awe of his positive transference feelings.

In the next instant, the patient's leg jerked violently and, for a moment, it seemed he might sit up (to regain a sense of volition over his bodily movement?). However, as it happened, he remained supine on the couch, motionless and silent for several minutes. When he spoke the patient sounded shaken, saying he had suddenly remembered a disturbing dream from the night before. He wondered why the dream had come to his mind at this moment and seemed to be struggling to orient himself to the occurrence in his dream and what was occurring in the session. Haltingly, he said that in the dream:

> A rodent was in my bed. I was terrified. I tried to call out to my wife but I couldn't make a sound. I guess I woke her up. I was looking around for the rodent. I was afraid to look under the covers and it took a while to realise that the rodent—or maybe it was a beaver— wasn't actually in our bed.

By exploring the sequence of the patient's libidinal transference and his involuntary leg movement, it became possible to understand the dream as an unconscious precursor to what was recapitulated in the session. The patient associated the rodent or beaver to his wife's leg, which he thought had probably brushed up against him while he was dreaming, resulting in confusion when he awoke about whether the animal was in his dream (internal) or in his bed (external). It seemed that something similar had happened in the session when he was sharing his loving feelings and then felt as if we—that is, patient and analyst—had *literally* touched, which both excited and frightened him. In this regard I felt that my patient was not only *remembering a dream* from the previous night but also *having a dream* in the session. That is, his involuntary leg movement and the sensations related to feeling physically in contact with the rodent/beaver/wife's leg gave him to feel, momentarily, that the analytic couch was the night-time bed in which he and his wife/analyst were together sleeping.

When the patient is thinking concretely, and reflective thinking is in abeyance (Britton, 1998, p. 73), technically it is important to avoid transference interpretations until the sensorial aspects of the experience are well contained. As the patient, for example, was able to describe where in the bed he thought the rodent lay, whether he saw it (he did not) or felt it moving around under the bedcovers, and what it was that made him think it was a beaver rather than another type of rodent, the sensorial elements of his experience were slowly transformed into increasingly complex, verbal thoughts and associations. The analyst's genuine curiosity in the patient's concrete experience is, I believe, containing and supports differentiation between psychic and external reality necessary for movement into the depressive position. In this regard I agree with Searles (1962, p. 576), who cautions that "It is a mistake to respond [to the patient's communication] in terms of its potential metaphorical meaning without first acknowledging its validity as a statement of literal fact." That is, the patient must first be able to successfully make contact with the analyst at the paranoid-schizoid level of experience, before facing anxieties attendant to approaching the depressive position. Aspects of experience—for example, my patient's wondering if the rodent in his dream was a beaver—that may eventually acquire symbolic significance, need first to be explored in their literal form. With this particular patient, an unhurried exploration of the somatic sensations experienced within the session and in his dream eventually allowed for the interpretation that feeling loved or touched, literally or figuratively, was as intense emotionally as feeling ignored (unloved) or untouched.

In concluding, I would like to offer this summary: the terms "concreteness" or "concrete thinking" are typically used in the psychoanalytic literature to denote a developmental stage preceding the capacity for metaphorical thinking, or to describe a regression from differentiation and mental growth. Concrete thinking, in this sense, is used as an antonym to metaphorical thinking. Alternatively, I suggest it is possible to observe a complementary relationship between concrete and metaphorical thinking that spurs normal development. Melanie Klein's theory of mental positions, as elaborated upon by Wilfred Bion and later by Ronald Britton, was utilised to show how psychic development may be thought of as resulting from ongoing oscillations between the normal paranoid-schizoid and depressive positions. Additionally, I propose that non-pathological concrete thinking can be considered part of the normal paranoid-schizoid position. If the disorganisation, lack of coherence, and uncertainty associated with this state of mind can be felt and contained, then new experience, at first represented literally, acquires metaphorical meaning as the next depressive position takes shape. As such, concreteness is not something that is overcome as the individual develops the capacity for metaphorical thinking. More accurately, concreteness grounded in sensory experience underpins metaphorical thinking. Clinical and non-clinical examples were provided to illustrate the essential features of this sensory-based form of thought, and to show its vital relationship to development. Implications for technique, including the importance of differentiating between pathological and non-pathological forms of concreteness and the containing function of the analyst's curiosity in, and respect for, the patient's concretely conveyed communications, were briefly mentioned.

If space allowed, I would be able to furnish many more examples of normal concreteness associated with the paranoid-schizoid position. Hopefully, the vignettes provided illustrate the ordinary quality of the experience and how it contributes to healthy development.

References

Bass, A. (1997). The problem of "concreteness." *Psychoanalytic Quarterly*, 66: 642–682.

Bion, W. R. (1963). *Elements of Psycho-Analysis*. London: Heinemann.

Bion, W. R. (1965). *Transformations*. London: Heinemann.

Bion, W. R. (1970). *Attention and Interpretation*. London: Tavistock.

Britton, R. (1998). Before and after the depressive position: Ps(n)→D(n)→Ps(n+1). In: R. Britton, *Belief and Imagination*. Hove, UK: Routledge.

Brown, L. (1985). On concreteness. *Psychoanalytic Review, 72*: 379–402.

Eliot, T. S. (1919). Hamlet and his problems. In: T. S. Eliot, *Selected Essays, 1917–1932*. New York: Harcort Brace, 1950.

Freud, S. (1896). Letter from Freud to Fliess, December 6, 1896. *The Complete Letters of Sigmund Freud to Wilhelm Fliess, 1887–1904*, pp. 207–214.

Freud, S. (1915e). The unconscious. *S. E.*, 14: 159–215.

Frosch, A. (1995). The preconceptual organization of emotion. *Journal of the American Psychoanalytic Association, 43*: 423–447.

Grossman, L. (1996). "Psychic reality" and reality testing in the analysis of perverse defenses. *International Journal of Psychoanalysis, 77*: 509–517.

Jacobsen, E. (1957). Denial and repression. *Journal of the American Psychoanalytic Association, 5*: 61–92.

Jones, E. (1916). The theory of symbolism. Cited in Segal, H. (1957). Notes on symbol formation. *International Journal of Psychoanalysis, 38*: 391–397.

Keats, J. (1817). Letter to George and Thomas Keats, December 22, 1817. London: Oxford University Press, 1952.

Keyes, R. (2006). *The Quote Verifier*. New York: St. Martin's Press.

Klein, M. (1930). The importance of symbol-formation in the development of the ego. *International Journal of Psychoanalysis, 11*: 24–39.

Klein, M. (1935). A contribution to the psychogenesis of manic-depressive states. In: M. Klein, *Love, Guilt and Reparation and Other Works, 1921–1945* (pp. 262–289). London: Karnac.

Klein, M. (1946). Notes on some schizoid mechanisms. In: M. Klein, *The Writings of Melanie Klein, Vol. III: Envy and Gratitude and Other Works, 1946–1963* (pp. 1–24). New York: Free Press.

Klein, M. (1955). On identification. In: M. Klein, *The Writings of Melanie Klein, Vol. III: Envy and Gratitude and Other Works, 1946–1963* (pp. 141–175). New York: Free Press.

Klein, M. (1959). Our adult world and its roots in infancy. In: M. Klein, *The Writings of Melanie Klein, Vol. III: Envy and Gratitude and Other Works, 1946–1963* (pp. 247–263). New York: Free Press.

Parnes, D. (2009). *Final Summary Paper for Infant Observation*. Unpublished paper written for Infant Observation at Northwestern Psychoanalytic Society, Seattle, WA.

Piaget, J. (1945). *Play, Dreams and Imitation in Childhood*. New York: W. W. Norton.

Piaget, J. (1954). *The Construction of Reality and the Child*. New York: Basic.

Poitier, S. (2008). *Life Beyond Measure*. New York: HarperCollins.

Poitier, S. (2009). Interview with Renee Montagne. NPR *Morning Edition*. KUOW, Seattle, WA. 19–20 May.

Renick, O. (1992). Use of the analyst as a fetish. *Psychoanalytic Quarterly*, *61*: 542–563.

Searles, H. (1959). Integration and differentiation in schizophrenia. In: H. Searles, *Collected Papers in Schizophrenia and Related Subjects* (pp. 304–316). Madison, CT: International Universities Press.

Searles, H. (1962). The differentiation between concrete and metaphorical thinking in the recovering schizophrenic patient. In: H. Searles, *Collected Papers in Schizophrenia and Related Subjects* (pp. 560–583). Madison, CT: International Universities Press.

Segal, H. (1957). Notes on symbol formation. *International Journal of Psychoanalysis, 38*: 391–397.

Notes

1. In using the term "object" I assume that the reader understands I am referring to both external others, such as the infant's primary cares, and to the many evolving internal representations of these relationships.

2. Klein elaborated Freud's concept of projection and offered the term "projective identification" to describe both unconsciously attributing unwanted aspects of the self to the object (1959, pp. 252–253) and unconsciously acquiring aspects of the object's identity then treated as part of the self (1955, pp. 141–175).

3. Britton (1998, p. 72) uses the term "regression" to refer exclusively to a pathological state of mind that "reiterates the past and evades the future". Regression is contrasted with the disorientation, emotional turbulence, and loss of coherence that accompanies relinquishment of the depressive position as one re-enters the paranoid-schizoid position. This latter experience is part of psychic development and as such should not be labelled as regression.

4. American visual artist Washington Allston first used the term "objective correlative" about 1840, but T. S. Eliot made it famous in his essay, *Hamlet and His Problems*, published in 1919.

5. Interestingly, the infant was actually tongue-tied and needed a minor medical procedure to allow for normal feeding. Thus, the observer is referring simultaneously to the concrete and metaphorical significance of the infant's and his own experience.

CHAPTER SEVEN

When words fail

Richard Lasky

This chapter will address how analytic treatment is facilitated when the inevitable stalemate occurs with a very commonly encountered but particularly difficult category of patient—the concrete patient who is not simply concrete but is also refractory to interpretation. The focus will be on why an entire category of patients are so concrete and are not helped by interpretation; about how the analyst, and analyst–patient transactions, and the analyst–patient relationship are internalised; and, on what specifically happens, within the broad range of those conscious and unconscious processes, that facilitates therapeutic action with this particular kind of difficult patient.

The patient: Mr V

Mr V came to treatment because he suffered from barely controllable rages that caused him many social and professional difficulties, including having turned almost all his friends, going back as far as he could remember, into enemies, wrecking every romantic relationship he ever had and, also, despite making a lot of money when he gets work, having been fired from every job he ever held. He recognised that he had a very serious problem, but he came with deep reservations about the ability of psychotherapy to be of help. He described asking everyone he knew for advice on how he might address his problem, and said he was told by the people he respected that psychoanalysis was the most comprehensive form of therapy. He was "willing to give analysis a crack at me", as he put it; "but I have to tell you", he went on, "that if this thing works it will be a miracle." His expectation of frustration and disappointment became understandable almost immediately.

Mr V's portrayal of his parents, his history, and his life was simple and it never varied. He was an only child and he described his mother as an overly intellectualised and self-involved college professor who was basically uninterested in him. She was a person who could not properly relate to him "because all she cared about was her work, never about people, and certainly not about me". Although Mr V had many such angry feelings about his mother, he retained few actual memories of her prior to her sudden, and unexpected, death just before he entered middle school. Mr V also claimed to have very few, almost no, memories of his childhood, and he found it difficult, when asked about his childhood or about his parents, to bring specific recollections intentionally to mind.

It turns out that Mr V actually did have memories, many memories, and some were quite vivid, in fact almost palpable, in their intensity. It was because of the form they took and the purposes they served that Mr V did not recognise, treat, or even experience his memories as memories. Mr V's memories were couched in chronic complaints levelled against his mother and, occasionally, his father. His inability to experience his complaints as a form of remembering was due, in part, to the concreteness of his thinking; memories were memories and complaints were complaints. Mr V also used these complaints as indictments, retaliatory denunciations that had the power both to injure and to redress injury. In addition to his concreteness, he resisted thinking about them as memories in order not to weaken their power as indictments. The litany of complaints directed against his mother (and to a lesser extent, his father) in session after session were, for Mr V, actual, not metaphorical, character assassinations. His denunciations of her were imbued, for him, with the retaliatory power to punish and destroy. Whenever I brought up the possibility, no matter how gently or tentatively, that his complaints might be more complicated than they seemed, Mr V would become furious with me; at such times he would tell me, in a voice tinged with steel, that he thought me a rather stupid person for not knowing the difference between a memory and a complaint, and he wondered how someone like me ever got into the business of doing therapy in the first place.

Mr V's history, or at least his version of it, which he could not readily convey as personal memories, emerged in the recounting of his complaints. For example: "On the rare occasion that my fucking mother turned her fucking attention to me, she found me always", he said, "to be just a great big fucking disappointment. That's it. That's the whole fucking picture. I never did anything fucking right, or fucking good enough, except, maybe, to take a fucking shit." The constant and repetitive use of the word "fucking" infiltrated almost everything Mr V said; he used it as a noun, a verb, and a modifier of virtually anything and everything. This illustrates another prominent and characteristic facet, a consequence actually, of what I will discuss more thoroughly at a later point, as Mr V's inadequately developed, as well as his degraded and defensive, use of language.

His furious statement that he could only do right by "taking a shit" was his shorthand way of commenting on a V family "legend": among all "the cousins" (there were seven children in his generation of the extended family), he was the one that was toilet trained the earliest; in fact, as the legend goes, he was mostly toilet trained by his first birthday and fully toilet trained not long after it. Everything Mr V knew about his toilet training he learned from the "legend"; it was not, as far as he knew, something he remembered. Being toilet trained so early was the only thing involving him that Mr V ever remembered his mother acknowledging with either a sense of pleasure or a measure of pride. As Mr V saw it, his mother boasted about his early toilet training as an achievement of hers, rather than his, and he could never even mention it without falling into a rage: "She always said that *she* toilet fucking trained me so young. Well, *I* was the one who was toilet fucking trained, not *her*. What did she fucking do to get so much fucking credit, huh? All she fucking did was make my fucking life fucking miserable unless I fucking did what she fucking said!"

Turning now to Mr V's father: he sounded like a chronically depressed, possibly alcoholic, and generally unavailable man, who aspired to be an artist but, after his marriage, was unable to make a successful living at it. His depression and withdrawal appears to have markedly increased on the heels of his wife's death. Mr V had nothing but contempt for his father, whom he described as "a schmuck, who wasted his fucking life" in a series of meaningless and unrewarding jobs. "He was a fucking failure," was how Mr V summed it up, whenever the topic of his father came up. Mr V also constantly felt misunderstood by his father, and said once, "Instead of talking fucking *to* one another, we talked fucking *past* one another." Despite the anger with which he always spoke about him, the lack of connection to his father seems to have been a source of frustration for Mr V. It was a painful absence that turned into what felt, to Mr V, like a complete abandonment of him after his mother's death. Mr V complained bitterly about how he "became an orphan" after her death, despite his conviction that neither of them really paid him any mind when she was alive. Mr V vehemently said, on more than one occasion, "I will feel deep fucking resentment toward them both for as long as I fucking live. If I live for-fucking-ever, that's how long I will fucking feel that way."

From the material thus far presented, and from bits and pieces collected over the course of his treatment, it appears that Mr V's mother was essentially as narcissistic with him during his infancy as she was described to be during the later years of his childhood. It seems quite likely that the scale of his rage, certain of his problems with reality-testing associated with a tendency towards action (specifically, an unconscious belief in the magical power of action), can be traced to excessive oral frustrations that prevented, or at the very least interfered with, the development of areas of the ego (and specific functions) that, with a more attuned mother, would have made the modulation of affects, frustration tolerance, and impulse control more possible. His mother's use of him, even as an infant, to regulate her own narcissistic pressures evoked chronically heightened states of tension that, since he was only an infant, he had no capacity to either regulate or diminish. That early experience may have been the template for his life-long condition of heightened affect within a chronic state of general over-stimulation, and it may also account for his chronic inability to manage the escalation of internal pressures in later life.

It is no surprise that narcissistic parenting raised, rather than reduced, conflicts and they then led to broad defects and deficits in ego development. Those early conflicts as well as the various impediments in function they caused were all greatly exacerbated, and the defensive structure he initiated in the oral stage acquired their distinctly anal colouration, when Mr V was driven, apparently quite traumatically, into such untimely urinary and bowel mastery. What came to have equal and, in some ways, even greater consequence for Mr V's current condition (and for his attempt at analytic work) were the injuries that further stunted and deformed his psychic development during the anal stage. In addition to the centrality and the critical impact of toilet training, we know that other important maturational requirements must also be mastered by toddlers, not least of which are the challenges of differentiation, separation, and individuation. Mr V's advancement into the anal-rapprochement phase created newer and more difficult problems for him. How to cope with the demands of this new phase when grievously unprepared in so many ways? How to negotiate it with grave ego weaknesses (with an ego that is deficient in some ways and defective in others)? How to traverse it lacking the defensive organisation that should have been available from a successful passage through the oral stage? And above all, how to negotiate all this with a highly narcissistic mother, poorly attuned to his needs? Many of Mr V's difficulties could be traced to the functional pathology that originated or was exacerbated during this period of his life. Among the many far-reaching developmental casualties that came to permeate his life, one in particular was a matter of real concern in contemplating his ability to make use of analysis. This was Mr V's inability to make use of the symbolising functions of words, speech, and language.

In the brief case material thus far presented, the anal-aggressive character of Mr V's language use is obvious as he inexorably infuses his speech with curses ("fucking" this, and "fucking" that) which may look either phallic or Oedipal because of their content but which are more closely related to a kind of angry anal smearing than anything else. The concreteness of his speech, and how very literal his speech is, is also readily apparent. We can see how poorly speech is distinguished from action by him, and also how much he seems to use speech as a form of action itself. And we have also seen to how great an extent his speech is used for gross tension relief and discharge purposes, rather than for the purpose of establishing a kind of communication intended to lead us together into a shared "analytic reality". But let us return now for some additional data, in order to focus on the disturbances in how Mr V made use of words, speech, and language, and on the implications it had for his treatment:

> Not long after Mr V entered treatment he told me the most amazing story. At some point between the ages of four and six, or perhaps

as late as seven, a paediatrician told Mr V's parents that his weight was on the high side of normal for a child of his size. The doctor went on to say that they might want to keep an eye on how he was eating, just to be sure that he remained within the normal range as he continued to grow. According to Mr V, his parents reacted dramatically to this information. They responded as if what they had been told was not that he was in the normal range, even if a bit near the high side, but that he was grossly, dangerously, disgustingly obese. They immediately began to treat him as if that were true; they commented negatively and incessantly on his appearance; they radically changed his diet; and they began to weigh him every morning and evening, and sometimes even in the afternoon, too.

Once during that time he was sent to live with his grandparents for seven weeks while his parents were off on a pleasure trip. Mr V said that according to an agreement between his parents and his grandparents, and much to his shock and dismay when his first mealtime arrived, he was to eat every meal separately from them, and they were to feed him only one meal per day. And that meal consisted of one cracker and one glass of water. He was to receive only seven crackers and seven glasses of water for each full week of the entire seven weeks of his stay with them. In all the times Mr V told this story he never described sneaking another cracker or glass of water when no one was looking. Mr V said that he never discussed this with his parents or his grandparents. He knew that if he raised the subject they would only tell him how fat and disgusting he was. He reported that when they returned from their trip, his parents resumed treating the issue of his weight exactly the way they did before they had left.

Mr V told that story over and over again in his treatment and no part of it ever changed. Mr V never wondered whether it was true; he never wondered whether he actually could have been fed a single cracker and only one glass of water a day, for seven weeks; he never wondered how he survived this without becoming ill; he never wondered why he had no memories of having lost weight as a result; he never questioned whether his grandparents really would have agreed to treat him that way; he never wondered how he knew what would happen if he asked his parents, or his grandparents, about this; and never did he express any doubt about the story or any part of it. In addition, he was never interested in their motives; he never wondered how they arrived at *one* cracker or one *cracker* per day, or how and why they settled on a single glass of water. Mr V never speculated about why his parents understood the paediatrician's information the way they did, or about why they reacted to it the way they did. Mr V was not interested, never even remotely curious, about the repetition of the number seven (seven cousins all told; being between four and six but perhaps as late as seven when the paediatrician spoke to his parents about his weight; seven years old when he stayed with his grandparents; and, the sevens that were repeated so frequently in the story itself—seven crackers each week, and seven glasses of water each week, for seven weeks). And, not least of all these, Mr V also never wondered why he brought that story up in treatment so frequently, or why he brought it up just when he did, or why he even brought it up at all.

Mr V's story was like a fly trapped in amber—a prehistoric tale, brought intact and unchanged from a frozen past, into a frozen present and future. The story may have been like a fly in amber, but his use of it was not. Mr V used his story like a multi-purpose tool or a "Swiss Army knife"; one of those things that have so many blades they can be used for anything and everything. For example: Mr V's preferred approach was to fill his hours with event reports, and the instant he caught himself drifting away from "hard facts" or if, in telling about something, he became aware of even the slightest indication of needing anything from me, he would immediately launch into the "crackers and water" story. If he had a memory of the past, the instant he realised that it was a memory in memory form, he would launch into the story. Complaining about his parents and his childhood was fine, but if he caught even the slightest hint of need or even nostalgia in what he was saying the story was soon to follow. There were many other occasions for telling the story but, to give just one more example, it was guaranteed to come up when he came in for a session and did not know what to talk about. Every account of his story was given fully charged with affect. And Mr V never tired of it, nor did he ever have anything to say about how frequently it came up.

Mr V's story was basically the same each time he told it. To him, that was the equivalent of telling it exactly the same way each time. If there was ever any variation, no matter how small, that I chose to comment about—for example, if he said "I was brought to stay with my grandparents" instead of the usual "sent to live" with them, and I wondered out loud about the wording change—Mr V would first become quite angry and then deeply confused about what I said. His behaviour with interpretations about this or anything else, no matter how non-confrontational, tentative, or well timed they were (from my point of view), received exactly the same treatment. He would not be able to remember exactly what I said or how I said it, and he would ask me over and over again to repeat parts of it. Soon he could not remember any of it, and he drew a complete blank when he tried to recall what I might have been talking about. This often escalated into his being unable to remember anything either of us had said, right from the moment he entered the room. The day after something like this he was likely to come in saying that just after he left yesterday, or just before he got here today, he finally "got" what I was talking about. He then would invariably misquote me, either in the main or entirely. Next, he would tell me his understanding of what I would have meant by what I said, if I had said what he said I said, instead of what I actually did say. I often felt with Mr V that I was forever trapped in the famous Abbot and Costello routine, "Who's on First"; and if this has become just a bit too confusing to easily follow for you, too, that was exactly the point. Usually within about ten minutes of Mr V's having "gotten" anything I said, he once again lost the memory of who said what and even what it was about. He would try to try to remember what he said, what I said, or the interpretation he had made of it earlier that session, but was never quite able to grasp it.

As is obvious by now, it would be something of an understatement simply to say that Mr V made attacks on linking. The violence with which he destroyed meaning, without seeming to suffer a formal thought disorder or an outright flight into psychosis, was characterological in nature rather than a defence that he could chose selectively, even if unconsciously, to employ. This was Mr V's reaction to almost anything I might say that went beyond a superficial comment with a clear link to the manifest content of his event report. The annihilation of meaning was by no means limited to potential conflicts I might stir up in him by making an interpretive comment, and attacks on linking were just as likely to appear in the most routine of our interchanges. Sessions easily could, and regularly did, deteriorate into these disorienting "Alice in Wonderland" kinds of interactions. It may not have happened with such prominence right from the start of Mr V's treatment, or I might not have been exposed to the repetitive nature of it enough to recognise it for what it was right from the start, or it is certainly possible that some countertransference reaction caused me to turn a blind eye to it. However, at some point during the first year of our work, the quantity and the tenacious adhesiveness of these reactions not only became apparent, they reached the point where they came to entirely dominate the treatment. Worse yet, when the nature of the problem did finally become clear to me, we had no way to work on it. Not surprisingly, at least in hindsight, Mr V would react in his characteristic way to any attempt I made to examine this very thing with him. Often, it is said, the simple fact of knowing what one is dealing with is more than half the battle won. That may be true for all kinds of problems but, in this case, because his reaction made it impossible for us to talk together about it, it was the way his treatment went for years.

When not furious, and not annihilating and obliterating meaning, Mr V was actually a very bright, articulate, and creative person. Because of time limitations I have not presented the many observable strengths that at first supported my thought that he might be able to benefit from analysis even though he had expressed reservations; over the years I have seen numerous instances of analyses that started with reservations and finished quite successfully. And beyond the initial strengths I saw, I have also left out other assets of his (and some were considerable, despite his difficulties). Given some of the strengths he had, if Mr V's problem was only that he tended to take umbrage too easily, that he often felt unfairly treated, that he experienced any difference of opinion as a personal attack (either on him, or by him), that he expected the worst in any situation, that he felt disappointments to be overwhelming, that he experienced frustration as torturously painful, that he had significant problems with affect regulation, that his object relations were essentially sadomasochistic, or that he had such a strong narcissistic current in his personality that he felt completely entitled to be brutally retaliatory with people he felt deserved it and did not give it a second thought afterwards (all of which were, in fact, true of him), there would still, even with that extensive list of difficulties, be no obvious or unequivocal reason why we could not, together, do the analytic work necessary to address those problems. To describe him in those terms alone actually would make him no different from many of the so-called "more difficult" patients that we regularly see in analysis today, and who do in fact end up getting considerable benefit from it.

Mr V's inability to use analysis effectively, the thing that makes him so different from those others, is because he was not just presented with conflict in his childhood (as they, and we, all are) but because he was overwhelmed by it; and not just inundated by conflict alone, but beset by it at a very crucial and decisive time. Mr V was flooded by unrelenting implacable conflict before, during, and after the crucial period in childhood when toddlers begin to develop the capacity to use words, speech, and language for symbolising purposes and as a symbolising process. I do not mean the simple acquisition of vocabulary, or the capacity to properly employ syntax and correct grammar; they can be learned and their uses are all possible even if the symbolising function of language is not present. And I do not simply mean the use of symbols, such as a cigar may stand for a penis or a purse may stand for a vagina, although that facility is certainly a part of the symbolising process. By the symbolising use of language I mean, for example, when words, when language, and when speech can be used to bind affect rather than only for the expression of it; I mean the ability to go beyond simply using them for discharge purposes; using words, speech, and language beyond the simple reduction of tension so that they can become instead the vehicle of genuine communication; I mean when words and speech can take the place of action, instead of being used as forms of action; when the use of language has the capacity to distil bodily tensions and sensations into modulated affect, or into thought, or into both modulated affect and thought simultaneously; and, above all, I mean when the availability of the symbolising function of language enables one to gain some degree of psychic distance from pure, unadulterated, unmodulated, raw, experience.

In considering the treatment of patients like Mr V my focus will be on the patient's internalisations of the analyst, the analyst–patient transactions, and the analytic relationship. I will describe how that can be achieved only by continuing to use verbal interpretation, if not directly for every intervention at least as the fulcrum for interventions with these patients. And I will explain the value in doing this despite the impediment these kinds of patients have with the functional use of words, speech, and language. Finally I will explain why, despite how paradoxical it appears to be, it is essential to engage in ongoing verbal interpretation throughout the analysis despite the fact that interpretations will not be likely to have mutative value for these patients until they are relatively close to the completion of the analysis. My focus on internalisation processes is not unique. Dorpat (1974, quoting Loewald, 1962) tells us that, "all analytic patients internalize patient-analyst transactions". I agree that this is a ubiquitous process with every patient, no matter how "difficult" or "easy", and I would only add the point that the more pronounced the pathology of the patient, the more critical the patient's internalisation processes will be in the conduct of an analysis.

I am aware of the seemingly contradictory nature of recommending a treatment that is based, to a considerable extent, on the sustained use of verbal interpretation with exactly the kind of patient who, at the very best, may only be able to understand the words that are used in an interpretation; who, if asked, could probably repeat the interpretation word for word; but who, nevertheless, is refractory to interpretation. I am also aware of how much more contradictory still it must seem to suggest doing exactly the same thing with the more extreme version of this kind of patient, that is with the kind of patient who cannot make sense of an interpretation, who cannot even take it in, and who could not repeat it back if his or her life depended on it; with the kind of patient who, at best, finds interpretations useless and, at worst, experiences interpretation not as a relief but as an active source of frustration or as an outright attack.

My approach to such patients has been informed by many of Loewald's (1960a, 1960b, 1962, 1970, 1973, 1979, 1986, 2007) ideas about what makes analysis possible, which I believe are equally applicable despite the vast difference between most of the patients he had in mind and the ones I am concerned with. I have also benefited greatly from his ideas about what makes an interpretation mutative, despite the fact that I am considering what kind of work can be done with patients for whom interpretation is either meaningless or useless. Loewald's views on internalisation processes in psychoanalysis are rooted in a model of the analytic dyad in which certain very critical ego identifications and superego identifications are taken on by the patient. Those identifications are not simple imitations, and when the process is functioning as well as we hope it will, those identification processes exist at extremely high levels of abstraction. From Loewald's point of view, identifications are not what bring about a cure and they are not the equivalent of (or an attempt to provide) a corrective emotional experience. He is suggesting instead that these identifications—not with the personal ego and superego of the analyst but with the analyst's analytic ego and the analyst's analytic superego—are essential ingredients in making the therapeutic environment (or what one might call the analytic situation) possible for patients. The safety of the analytic environment cannot be taken for granted by anyone, and it is especially not a given for patients like

Mr V; it may be the starting point from which everything else proceeds, but it requires extensive analytic work, often over many years, before its safety can be established with patients at that level or with that kind of pathology. The ability to bring in to treatment actively conflictual material, to expose wishes that are unacceptable, forbidden desires, and terrible, sickening fears, everything that is strenuously defended against in order to block them from ever emerging into consciousness, is close to impossible even for neurotic patients with fully adequate symbolising functions and complete mastery of verbal expression. It is an astronomical order of magnitude harder for patients like Mr V; however, he and all the others, no matter where they fall on the spectrum of psychopathology, facilitate their experience of the analytic situation as safe enough to confront these things not by reality testing but through an unconscious process of internalisation. Loewald suggests that a partial substitution of the analyst's analytic superego can alter the patient's superego in much the same way that a teacher can assume the moral authority of a parent when a child is first sent to school. And it is the result of this identification altering the patient's superego, not a takeover but a subtle retuning of the superego, that enables the patient to allow material that is ordinarily disavowed and warded off to arise into the preconscious and then, finally, to emerge into consciousness for exposure to analytic work.

In considering the degree of attunement necessary to make interpretations, Loewald draws on the mother-infant analogy. Loewald is concerned with shaping the communication in such a way that, just as happens with a mother and her baby, it accurately complements the patient's capacity to take it in. In his analogy the baby, experiencing undifferentiated painful levels of tension, learns to differentiate and identify the differences, for example, between wanting to be held but not necessarily fed and wanting to be fed and not only held. I will extend this analogy in order to suggest what I think happened over the course of many years to have made analysis actually useful for Mr V (and you must have guessed that it turned out to be, otherwise why would I be writing this chapter?). When the baby recognises from its mother's behaviour that it wants to be fed, not picked up, or picked up but not necessarily fed, we would say that the mother has communicated the contents of her ego to the baby by getting what her baby needs right, first through trial and error but after that, again and again, in a systematic way. Over and over again, these experiences take place and, eventually, when the baby has learned the differences and knows what it wants, we would say that the contents of the baby's ego are reflecting the contents of the mother's ego. By the time the baby can imagine satisfaction as a way of tolerating the time it takes for the mother to come and actually satisfy those needs, among the many things we might say about denial, hallucinatory wish fulfilment, magical thinking, narcissistic omnipotence, the omnipotence of the wish, etc., we would also say that an identification has taken place; we would say that the contents of the baby's ego exist through identification with the contents of its mother's ego.

There is, however, something else that is happening here which is of even more importance; that is, through the baby's observation of its mother, another, different, and infinitely more important identification is taking place. As the baby takes in what is happening, however much primitive perception and immature cognitive processes permit, the baby sees the mother at first struggling to figure out what is bothering her baby, what her baby needs. This is not something she knows automatically as a result of hard-wired signals between the two of them that make it unmistakable. In fact, the mother makes mistake after mistake, getting it wrong at first much more often than getting it right, and that is not just something the baby sees but something the baby experiences, until finally the mother comes to recognise the cues in her baby and cues in the environment that make the baby's needs comprehensible to her. But this is not all; if the mother understands what the baby needs but does not deal with it correctly, the baby does not learn what it needs to, or what it is supposed to, from the interaction. For example if, instead of feeding baby when that is what it needs (and not feeding but holding baby when that is what it needs), she says to her newborn infant instead, "You know Sweetie Pie, you have two kinds of cries, one for being fed and one for being held, and this is the one you use when you want to be fed," there is no way imaginable that this baby will get anything beyond intense frustration and increased agitation from her behaviour. The mother has to respond properly for the baby to get what it needs psychologically from this. But even when she is on the right track she still will not get it right immediately or even all of the time. The baby will witness the mother's trial and error attempts to satisfy its needs in a way that is appropriate not just to its needs but also to its abilities, until she finally can get all of this right most of the time. In this process the baby will be witnessing its mother's ego at work;

not just the contents, held versus fed, but the struggle to comprehend it all—what it is that is happening, what has to be done about it, how does it have to be done for it to be done right—everything that needs to be understood and done. The baby will not only identify with the contents of its mother's ego, it will also identify with the functions of its mother's ego, that is, with the ego as a structure that makes sense out of things, that takes action when needed, that figures out what kind of action is best. I am suggesting that patients with immature, damaged, or deformed egos, in witnessing their analyst's attempt to understand and help them, are able to take in not only the contents of their analyst's ego during that process but also can make use of the much more important internalisation of their analyst's analytic ego as a functional structure, as a substitute and, over the passage of considerable time, as the model for their own now repaired ego in much the same way as I just presented in the analogy.

The analyst is never passive in the treatment. The analyst is constantly struggling to understand what is going on, is working hard, all the time, to make some kind of reasonable sense out of what happened to this patient or is happening at the present moment in the treatment, and why. The patient is unable to communicate sufficiently, so that the analyst struggles constantly, and almost in isolation because it is so one-sided, with what happened to this person to create such difficulties. Where did this pathology start, why is it so severe, why this kind of pathology in particular? What strengths does this person have; how did the strengths develop, why these particular strengths? What does that story mean: is it a memory of something that actually happened; is it a memory of what the patient wished would have happened; is it a memory that is the opposite of what happened; is it a memory of what the patient was afraid would happen; is it a memory of something else entirely; is it a screen memory; is it a memory that is changed specifically to allow the patient to be in an active position instead of being forced to be a passive victim; is it not a memory at all; is it pure fantasy, and, if so, to what end; is it actually multiple fantasies or multiple memories represented by this single memory; is this the product of innumerable reorganisations of fantasy? And, what is it that is behind these constantly shifting, always larger than life, versions of me that the patient experiences; or behind this impossibly static and eviscerated version of me that the patient constantly experiences? And, what just took place in the patient's mind to cause what just happened between us; or is it because the patient registered the presence of something that just happened in my mind, and misunderstood what it was; or is it because something just happened between the two of us that I completely missed, let alone made proper sense of? The analyst struggles with understanding in this way, trying to make some kind of reasonable sense out of these kinds of things, for years; and throughout all that time the analyst is always doing this in the presence of the patient. It matters little whether the patient uses the couch, sits up, or paces the room as the analyst engages in this ongoing struggle because it is not just what the patient sees, nor is it only what the patient hears, nor is it particularly what the patient can read about the analyst's unconscious at any given moment; it is the apperceptive reception, everything that impinges from every possible source that will register over time, the manner in which all ways of experiencing become melded in the patient's experience of the analyst's struggle to understand the patient that will come to have the power to imprint something meaningfully different in the patient's mind. The patient is also the witness, the apperceptive recipient, of the analyst's constant struggle to find ways that will help the patient to understand these things, to find a way to help the patient gain perspective, to examine inner experience, and to acquire a meaningful understanding of both current and past experience. And this is why a retreat from talking to the patient analytically must not happen. Wishes, fears, defences, transference, resistance, all that and everything else analytic needs referencing as analytic throughout the work. It does not matter what modifications in the traditional frame may have been necessary in the course of the analysis, they must be talked about analytically. It does not matter how much or how little support has been necessary, nor does it matter what kind or for how long, it must all be talked about analytically. It does not matter how damaged a patient's functional use of words, speech, or language may be, to turn away from analysis in favour of uninterpreted support will, whatever immediate problem in the treatment it is intended to solve, end up depriving the patient of infinitely more than anything that could possibly be gained by it.

It took more than a decade, but Mr V eventually did make gains in his treatment; in fact, gains that were as significant as any reasonable person could wish from analysis. That was the evidence and the proof of my assertion that continuous meaningful verbal interpretation was not lost on Mr V, nor is it lost on patients like him; and, while it remains undeniably true for most patients of this kind that interpretations take on their greatest analytic power near the end of their analyses, interpretations are, throughout, what enable the end of an analysis to ever come into sight.

What is striking in Mr V's positive outcome was his eventual ability to use interpretation. I have attempted to describe the kinds of unconscious internalisation processes that allowed Mr V to acquire the symbolising function of language, words, and speech; and the analytic conditions that facilitated those internalisation processes, which led to his being able to use at first my interpretations, and eventually his own interpretations, thoughts, and ideas to better understand himself. I see this as a transformative interpersonal experience that fosters intrapsychic maturity; it is an internalisation process that affects a patient's functional capacities which then, through further sublimation, becomes a dynamic property of autonomous unconscious mental life that ordinarily remains available forever. For Mr V this became possible because I did not favour support (the attempt to manage indisputably problematic functioning) over trying to progressively understand him; and because I accompanied whatever I thought I understood, always, with a constant effort to find a way of using words, however difficult that appeared to be, to express that understanding to him in a way that was meaningful to him, not just to me. Support, as contrasted with interpretation, employs action; and support does not exclude how one uses words, because the supportive use of words means using them as a form of action (for example, in reassurance designed to calm or soothe rather than to convey deeper understanding). The necessity of support is unquestioned in the treatment of many very disturbed patients, but my point is that when the preverbal/nonverbal nature of the patient's mental processes, the deep impairment in the patient's functional and symbolising use of language, words, and speech, causes the analyst to despair of interpretation, the necessary support then becomes an end in itself; and the end having been achieved, there is no longer any reason to talk further about it. In this, the very best one can possibly hope for, even with the most positive outcome, is a transference cure. There are many reasons why a person may not be able to develop the ability to use insight, no matter how doggedly the analyst hews to interpretation: severity of pathology (Mr V's degree of pathology is by no means the ultimate possible), overwhelming traumatic injury leading to ineradicable psychic scarring or destruction, and low intelligence, are among the most obvious. A transference cure is nothing to scoff at for people who are genuinely incapable of structural change. Let us make no mistake about this: for many people in that position it can change a hellish existence into a life worth living. But I am trying to make a distinction here between something intrinsic in the patient and something the analyst does, that is, the analyst's abandonment of consistent analysis, however well meaning, that ultimately may limit the outcome to a transference cure. As wonderful as a transference cure may be for some, the benefits that structural change confers on those who are capable of achieving it are vastly superior. Anything short of genuine structural change would have short-changed Mr V. In current practice we are regularly presented with pathology that seems so very deep and seems to so infiltrate the patient's personality that we are tempted to think of the modifications that may be necessary rather than the analysis that may be possible. That is certainly understandable, but it should not become so automatic a response that it turns out to be us, rather than the patient, who are unable to analyse.

References

Dorpat, T. (1974). Internalization of the patient-analyst relationship in patients with narcissistic disorders. *International Journal of Psychoanalysis*, 55: 183–188.

Loewald, H. (1960a). On the therapeutic action of psychoanalysis. *International Journal of Psychoanalysis*, 41: 16–33.

Loewald, H. (1960b). Internalization, separation, mourning, and the superego. *Psychoanalytic Quarterly*, 31: 483–504.

Loewald, H. (1962). The superego and the ego-ideal. *International Journal of Psychoanalysis*, 43: 264–268.

Loewald, H. (1970). Psychoanalytic theory and the psychoanalytic process. *Psychoanalytic Study of the Child*, 25: 45–68.

Loewald, H. (1973). On internalization. *International Journal of Psychoanalysis*, 54: 9–17.

Loewald, H. (1979). Reflections on the psychoanalytic process and its therapeutic potential. *Psychoanalytic Study of the Child*, 34: 155–167.

Loewald, H. (1986). Transference–countertransference. *Journal of the American Psychoanalytic Association*, 34: 275–287.

Loewald, H. (2007). Internalization, separation, mourning, and the superego. *Psychoanalytic Quarterly*, 76: 1113–1133.

CHAPTER EIGHT

Some observations about working with body narcissism with concrete patients

Janice S. Lieberman

In the recent documentary film *Valentino, the Last Emperor*, the great fashion designer asked (as did Sigmund Freud a century ago): "What does a woman want?" The answer was simple for Valentino, but not for Freud. "A woman wants ... to be beautiful." I think that Valentino had it right on many levels. The wish to be beautiful is true of many women. Many men too want to be handsome, and many men want to be with a woman who is beautiful. Psychoanalysis has had little to say about the wish for beauty, yet it dominates the thoughts of so many.

In my private practice in New York I have found that increasing numbers of patients present initially or after some months of psychoanalytic treatment with preoccupying concerns about bodily and/or facial appearance. They do not understand their anxiety about these issues to be "symbolic" of anything. Although they are intelligent and may be able to understand other feelings about other issues in more abstract ways, their worries and questions about the importance of their looks are concrete, and so is the language they use. One university professor confessed that: "When I look in the mirror, I am not sure of what I see and I need someone to tell me what they see."

Many of today's patients suffer from developmental deficits lingering from childhood. They were not really "seen"; they were incorrectly "seen"; or they were falsely mirrored. They do not as adults really know what they look like and are vulnerable to being shamed, humiliated on a bodily level. The body image is not constant. (We have coined the term "object constancy" but not "body constancy"!) These patients come into treatment with enhanced body awareness accompanied by enhanced shame, self-consciousness, and a profound need for attention given to their bodies. Many do not have sexual relations or have sex infrequently, shame being an inhibitor, or in some cases shame functions as a defence against the experiencing of sexual feelings.

Disturbances in body narcissism are often reflected in more or less temporary disturbances in the capacity for metaphoric language when speaking about the body, its appearance, and its maintenance. It is my thesis that psychoanalysts should not "rush to metaphor" as they have been trained to do when making interpretations, but rather, they should "linguistically attune" to such patients. Concrete responses from the analyst about his or her observations of the patient's body issue in question, of what is revealed at the level of the skin and clothing, actually facilitate the patient's capacity for symbolic thinking. Such responses repair the narcissistic deficit underlying the preoccupation, allowing the ego to grow and further develop.

When Freud wrote in 1923 that the ego is first and foremost a bodily ego, I believe that he was referring to an *inner* experience of the body. The patients I speak of here refer to: (1) their external bodies as seen from the outside by themselves in the mirror—the body's size, shape, muscle tone; and (2) from the inside, by their own critical internalisations. Freud's neglect of the external, visually understood body was explained by Gilman: "Freud's intellectual as well as analytic development in the 1890s was a movement away from the 'meaning' of visual signs ... to verbal signs, from the crudity of seeing to the subtlety of hearing" (1995, p. 22). Gilman (1998) also wrote that "Freud stopped seeing the outside to [sic] the body as a means of judging the inner workings of the psyche and focused on the invisible and unseeable aspects of the psyche." He now saw the fantasy as the source for the types of physical ailments that manifest themselves in sexual dysfunction and hysteria" (p. 93). Freud did not like his own looks. He did not like to be photographed and he made faces when he was. His mother's vanity might have influenced his championing a "talking cure" rather than a "looking cure".

Another twentieth century intellectual, Jean-Paul Sartre, regarded himself as the victim of the look. As Jay (1993) noted: "The body looked at was to Sartre a fallen object subject to the mortifying gaze of the other" (p. 22). Mirrors were fraught with danger for Sartre and for Freud too. In *The Uncanny* (1919h) Freud reported an overnight train ride in which a mirrored door opened and an elderly man in a dressing gown came in. Freud thoroughly disliked the man's appearance. Then he realised that it was his own image in the mirror. Freud never mentioned in the Wolf Man case what Brunswik (1928), the Wolf Man's second analyst noted. According to Brunswik, the Wolf Man "neglected his daily life because he was so engrossed, to the exclusion of all else, in the state of his nose", its supposed scars, holes, and swelling: his life centered on the mirror in his pocket, and his fate depended on what it revealed or was about to reveal" (see Phillips, 1996, p. 19).

Whether they did so in Freud's time or not, many of today's patients come into psychoanalytic treatment feeling ashamed about the way they look, whether the shame has to do with the entire body or it parts: arms, legs, face, nose, lips, hair, body fat, acne scars, tallness, shortness, etc. Others are ashamed of the way their lovers or spouses or parents look. Most psychoanalysts, in classical Freudian tradition, pay little attention to these concrete complaints, assuming that they are manifest content and derivatives of inner dynamics, compromise formations. I have found that working with patients who are ashamed of their bodies by interpreting what I assume must be the underlying fantasies and meanings of the shame either hits a stone wall of non-comprehension or in some cases, meets with intellectual compliance with the interpretation, but little alteration of the shame experience.

I see shame as a painful and powerful affect suffered early on at a time when the child lacked the words that would have made the shame experience more bearable and metabolisable. In addition, the bodily and social vicissitudes of early adolescence force one to revisit these early affects and combine with them to produce the language-deficient shame we see in our consulting rooms with adults. Jacobs (2005) has recently postulated the "adolescent neurosis" as equal to or even more important than the "infantile neurosis". He speaks about early adolescence and its bodily disharmony (ages eleven to fourteen) and notes that it is quite difficult to retrieve memories of shame about the body from this time, the teasing and exclusion by peers, because the young adolescent does not have the capacity for metaphoric thought that the later adolescent has.

As I emphasised in my (2000) book *Body Talk: Looking and Being Looked at in Psychotherapy*, the body is a concrete object with an actual concrete manifestation and actual physical feelings (as opposed, say, to an idea or a fantasy). We have to begin to deal with our bodies well before the emergence of abstract thought … therefore, psychological issues about the body appear to require a concreteness of thought other issues do not. I have found that concrete thinking is often connected with problems in the development of the bodily self and its boundaries, and is connected with early deficits in attention to the body, its care, and maintenance. Such problems intersect and interact with the development of inner fantasy, conflict, and defence from early childhood on.

It has been a decade since I published that book, and I have been able to fine tune my thinking about the relationship between bodies and language due to a plethora of articles and books recently published that confirm and add to my theories. (Among them are Farrell, 2000; Lombardi, 2003, 2008; Mitrani, 2007; and Steiner, 2006.) When I researched my book, I missed the important work of Rizzuto (1988) who noted that: "Psychoanalytic theorizing has not paid enough attention to the function of language in the development of character structure, transformation of object relations, but most important, regulation of affect and self-esteem" (p. 2). She has observed that "The avoidance of communication seems to be a defence against the transference. For these patients, *that is the transference*" (p. 4).

Several recent cases both in psychoanalysis and psychotherapy have provided me with more insight into the underpinnings of body narcissism. I have had to think more about the role of shame due to my presentation on a panel on Shame and the Body in New York with Riccardo Lombardi in March 2006. The writings of others have helped me to analyse my countertransference reactions, potentially powerful and disruptive to treatment. In my work with these patients, I have had to tolerate exposure to abject bodily processes and have had to think about and talk about them. I have had to tolerate constant cycles of need and rejection, provocations to withdraw from the treatment in transference/countertransference cycles that repeat the early relationship with the mother.

I will present to you three case examples.

First case vignette

Amanda, a thirty-five-year-old marketing executive, was referred to me for psychoanalytic treatment by the analyst she saw while in college.

She had relocated to New York at the age of twenty-five, but had not "psychologically" separated from her mother, with whom she was in cell phone and e-mail contact many times a day. Her parents had been divorced since Amanda was nine. Her mother was their "mainstay". Her father, considered to be quite "crazy", was essentially unavailable. Her mother would stay in a hotel, visiting for a month at a time. Mother's visits (as well as phone calls and e-mails) involved constant negotiations about money. I had the feeling that Amanda wanted to suck her mother dry.

Although I had been told by the referring analyst that Amanda had a serious eating disorder, an attractive, trendily dressed young woman swept into my office. She may have seemed anorectic elsewhere, but was more normal by New York standards. The referring analyst thought she was a virgin still. Amanda reported living with James, an architect, who adored her and who listened to all her complaints, soothing her endlessly as he did his mother. He barely earned a living and Amanda was angry that she was their main support. She also described James as a "baby" who could not handle the simple matters of life; it seemed clear to me that she wished that she could trade places with him as the one who played "baby".

Amanda told me that she sought treatment to keep her resolution to do "good things" to her body. She wanted to become pregnant and had been told that she might not be able to do so because she had not menstruated in eight months, or very much before that, for that matter. She told me that after a boyfriend jilted her at the age of sixteen she became anorectic and had to be hospitalised for a while. Since then her diet was vegetarian only and she had little appetite for many foods. She was an internet addict, researching every food she ate for problems. I detected considerable grandiosity ("I can only eat the best") as well as paranoia in this matter.

As treatment began, Amanda began to visit a series of dermatologists and was particularly upset by one who "assaulted" her by biopsying several small bumps on her chest. She experienced this as a kind of rape. (The displaced negative transference was thus activated.) On some level I believe that she was experiencing me as attacking her and invading her, but she protected herself from awareness of this through displacement.

Amanda had a slight case of acne and became obsessed with it. She stood in front of the mirror for hours looking at and squeezing the pimples, thus making the irritation worse. She tried all kinds of creams on her face, then looked up their ingredients on the internet, concluding that they were "bad" for her. She argued with each dermatologist about the safety of the creams and antibiotics they prescribed. She came to me as "referee" and spent countless hours with her mother on the phone about whether these products would cause her permanent damage. (Her mother seemed to share similar concerns about her own body.) Amanda was concerned that with her anorexia and her treatment for acne she had done "permanent" damage to herself, had caused permanent scars.

A classic understanding of her problems would be one of castration anxiety and fears of genital damage. My treatment of her was along the lines described in my (2000) book: I spoke with her quite concretely, since she was unable to speak of her issues as if they had any psychological meaning. She wanted me to see her face each session and to let her know what I thought: was it better or worse? She came in suffering. "I've had a miserable weekend. I have driven my boyfriend and my mother crazy." I thought that she wanted to drive me crazy too. She burst into tears the way a two-year-old might do. In addition to the dermatologists she visited, Chinese herbalists, acupuncturists, and cosmeticians were called on to look at her and give their opinions. She challenged every suggested treatment. I was called upon as another "mirror" to try to soothe the bad image she had of herself. She would come in and confess (in a highly dramatic manner): "I was BAD", meaning that she had picked her pimples. It was high drama, and I was quite aware of the role I had been cast in. I was also willing to play that role, since it confirmed the hypotheses I had developed about working with body narcissism. The kind of aversive countertransference I might have had fifteen years prior ("I cannot believe that I am listening to such rubbish!") was quite muted due to my experience with so many of these patients, what I regard as the patients of our time.

A concurrent scenario was being played out on the gynaecological end as Amanda sought treatment for what she imagined to be her "infertility". She had been told as a young girl by a doctor her mother had taken her to that she would have problems conceiving a child. She pitted several traditional medical doctors against several Chinese doctors. This daughter of divorce trusted no one. She was afraid that the hormones the medical doctor prescribed would damage her eggs and that the herbs given her by the Chinese doctor had aggravated her acne.

I continued to look at her face as she came in and commented about the redness or lack thereof of her pimples. I asked her if she had picked them. My concrete interventions and my taking her complaints seriously began to calm her down after many weeks. She needed reassurance that she had not permanently damaged her face or body. I did not offer it but did offer attention and talking. My task, as I saw it, was to look, to be verbally descriptive, affirming, and to avoid any seductive or personal, non-professional compliments or vocal intonations.

I used my psychoanalytic lens to understand what was going on underneath. She was quite conscious of envying a pregnant friend, the envy being so great that she could not see her friend any more. As is my custom from time to time to test the current level of my patients' thinking, I tried a metaphoric statement: "The bumps on your face may represent baby bumps." She had no response to this, as if it were nonsense. At another time, I interpreted, "Picking your face is a substitute for picking on yourself," but this too went nowhere with Amanda.

Somehow the traditional medical doctor's advice prevailed and Amanda took antibiotics and then progesterone for a week. At her check-up she was told that she was pregnant. (In the transference, in which she was a needy child, no mention of sexual relations had been made.) Fleeting moments of pleasure about this fact were soon turned to pain and worry as Amanda feared she had already damaged her baby with the various creams she was putting on her face for her acne as well as whatever was in the little food she was eating. Her visits to the dermatologists now included her obsessive questioning about the safety of their products for pregnant women. They reassured her, but she then found on the internet that they were not "safe". Her fears of damaging herself then morphed to damaging her baby. She stayed in the house at the weekends because she did not want to be seen with acne.

Concurrent with the treatment in which she was quite regressed, Amanda was working in a very challenging job. She received a considerable salary raise during this time. Her job required a high level of interpersonal as well as other skills. She and her boyfriend kept appointments with the doctor who was to deliver her baby (although she had a second one waiting in the wings.) She consulted with a nutritionist about prenatal nutrition and brought in to her sessions bags of "healthy" food to show me she was taking care of herself in this way. I believe that the transference reflected a regression in body narcissism that had to be worked through with me as a kind of verbal mirror, continually reflecting back to her what I saw.

Although her mother seemed to be quite attentive to Amanda as an adult, there is some evidence of severe neglect when she was a young child. She has a memory of having broken a glass at the age of four. Her mother did not have the resulting torn finger repaired properly. One can only wonder what fantasies emanated from this, e.g., castration fears. When in treatment with her former analyst, Amanda developed psoriasis on that very finger, and the analyst interpreted her somatisation as due to that trauma. She remembered after many months having to wear a metal bar that connected her shoes while she slept, a method used to correct a slightly displaced hip. When she asked her mother about it, her mother could not remember it.

From the transference I have concluded that Amanda was a needy and annoying child who her mother tried to appease and then ignore. Her pregnancy gave her the excuse to not return to her home town that summer. She feared being seen with the acne.

Although she had quite a distance to travel to my office by subway, Amanda came to her sessions until the week she was to give birth. Her skin seemed miraculously better, for she had ceased aggravating it with picking. She was excited and looking forward to the birth process. "Squeezing the baby out" was my metaphor, a replacement for squeezing her skin.

She sent me an e-mail and photos of her lovely baby daughter Emily and was proud of having a quick delivery and natural childbirth. She planned to nurse Emily. Her mother arrived to help her out for the first month. Amanda enjoyed the breastfeeding, but Emily developed colic and screamed for several weeks. When she was three months old, Amanda brought the baby to my office. She seemed quite comfortable caring for her in my presence, nursed her, and was very proud to display her skills as a mother, her child's lovely outfit, and her own white, unblemished face. She had to resume her job on a part-time basis and hoped to continue sessions. I did not hear from her for several months, somewhat of a surprise to me, since she had seemed so attached to her treatment.

Prior to my summer vacation that year, I received a frantic call from Amanda. She had hired a nanny to take care of Emily and the nanny was quite critical of her continuing to nurse at eight months. She felt that the baby was not getting enough food. Amanda said that the paediatrician was not unhappy—the baby was in the fortieth percentile in weight. She was leaving in a few weeks for a month in her home town. Her ninety-two-year-old grandmother might die if she did not come, as she put it. Six weeks later, she returned, speaking in her session as if she had never left. It seemed that the nanny had been the recipient of strong negative (and some positive) transference feelings. Amanda was hysterical over fears that a man she had paid $500 to put in a water filter was not trustworthy. She feared that the water in her apartment was not safe for the baby. Although there might have been a slight reality to her concerns, it was apparent to me that the visit to her family had reawakened her paranoid anxieties. As she reconnected with me, she began to calm down. Her language was no longer concrete as she spoke about feeling that she had to respond instantly to her baby's cries and did not want to work to earn money so she could give her good care. She was having difficulty dealing with her daughter's demands (as her own mother had), and her own greediness in demanding money from her mother was coming to the surface. It seemed to me that the anxieties about her acne were defending against the material that was now emerging.

Second case vignette

Shame about her body affected my patient Wendy's willingness to engage in sexual relations. It became at certain times in the treatment the predominant theme. Wendy at thirty began an analysis after her brief marriage ended in divorce. She also had had relationship difficulties with men, her parents, her brothers, women friends, and her bosses at work. She hoped through the treatment to better understand herself, to remarry, and to find a better job. Oedipal rivalry with her mother, masochistic revenge and surrender to her mother, penis envy, and low self-esteem about being a girl were strong components of her psychic development. When she spoke about her relationship difficulties she was highly articulate and able to grasp the meanings of her difficulties in terms of her inner conflicts as we knew them from the analysis of her infantile fantasy life, her early memories, her dreams, and the transference.

I will tease out from these other issues the kinds of shameful issues Wendy spoke of from time to time, focusing on them for weeks or months: her body and bodily processes, of which she was ashamed and contributed to her feeling like an outcast. An early dream made it apparent that she experienced her body as a messy kitchen drawer. When in this state of mind Wendy would walk into my office with her head turned to avoid my eyes and left the same way. She feared underarm odour, sweated a lot, and wore dress shields, which made her even warmer. Her sweat or odour were never manifest. Wendy was slender with a boyish figure, but complained that she was too fat, that her legs and thighs were thick and that her body had ugly cellulite on it that no man would want to look at. Her breasts were too small—her brothers got penises but the compensatory breasts she had hoped for never grew.

She had numerous childhood and adolescent memories that buttressed the reality for her of her bodily shame. She told me these stories over and over. As a child, when she sneezed, she honked and long snot emerged. Her brothers called her a snot-nosed snotter (and as an adult, despite this shame, or perhaps because of it, her behaviour could be most aptly described as "snotty"). Her mother forced her to do exercises to reduce her thighs when she was a teenager. At college the boys hung up a ham hock in honour of her "thunder thighs". It took years in treatment for her to wear tailored trousers: there was little reality to this shameful perception of herself, for she wore size six. Her other chronic complaint was her shame over having "nothing to wear". She did not know what clothes to buy, spent her weekends in the stores, bought clothes she loved for an hour, then hated them, and had to return them.

Wendy recalled her mother, who died a few years into her treatment, as always elegantly dressed and slender, taking her shopping, trying to force clothes on her that she did not want. Her mother was not tuned to what she needed for her body to feel right and therefore Wendy was unable to do so for herself. She barely listened to my words for many years. She could not bear to hear me speak and would shout that I was interrupting her. It was apparent, however, that she needed me desperately: she never missed a session and always came on time, never missing a minute, let alone a session. Nevertheless she denigrated me. I was a "nothing", just like her. Several years into the treatment and having worked with a number of patients who were ashamed of their bodies, I found a way to work with Wendy:

W: I never feel that I look that great. I never know what to wear. I am so uncomfortably warm today.

A: It is 90 degrees out. Yet you are wearing a wool cardigan and slacks. What about that?

Wendy's deepest dread of sweating and smelling was getting close to realisation by her garb. I made a mundane statement that addressed a concrete reality that I saw before me. I showed her that I was looking at her bodily rather than thinking about the "meaning" of her words. (Warm because of sexual feelings heating up? Wanting me to find her looking great and fishing for a compliment? That is, the more classical explanations and interpretations.)
    Then:

W: I have to go to a business lunch tomorrow at the Four Seasons and I have no idea of what to wear. I will feel humiliated.
A: You could pass by there today and see what people are wearing.

My interventions, concrete and mundane, and linguistically attuned to the level of Wendy's language in those sessions, were informed by several years of analytic work with Wendy. I had come to the conclusion that there had been a profound lack of loving and caring maternal attention to her body and bodily needs and, especially, a lack of verbalising about what was *seen*. My concrete statements addressed the consequent deficits I had observed in Wendy's capacity to care for herself. My comments were available for understanding on two levels: the concrete one of which she was at that time capable, and the historical/metaphorical one (sexual heat in the transference; not looking at others due to the pain of envy, suppression of curiosity) in which I had encoded my understanding of her childhood experience.
    A series of interventions such as these, in which my looking at her was evident in my words to her, resulted in Wendy's purchasing a stylish wardrobe, feeling good about her body, and slowly she began to return to working symbolically and metaphorically in the analysis. We once again focused on issues of envy and revenge, punishment for competitiveness, etc. Wendy's fantasy life was Medea-like in the extent of its violence.

The smooth course the analysis then took was threatened when Wendy became involved in an automobile accident and badly injured her neck and back. She barely missed a session, however. She needed to talk about her body and what was happening to it. She reported in assiduous detail her numerous hospital and doctor examinations and tests and her numerous physical therapies. Any residual shame was countered by the gratification she received having so many professionals look at her body and talk with her about every aspect of it. She then came to her sessions and told me word for word what they said. A more consolidated body image was thus reached by way of this unfortunate event, the car accident. As Caper (1994) so well put it: "The mind needs reliable information about itself—truth, if you will, just as the body needs food." I would add, so does the body need reliable information about itself.

As I wrote in *Body Talk*: "I believe that children who do not master this first level of language—the description of their own body parts and those of others—along with its necessary intrinsic connection with body awareness, vision and mother herself, are likely to suffer as adults from deficits in the consolidation of the body image" (p. 67). Today I would add: "and from proneness to shame".

This is true of those in middle age, who experience a second adolescence. How poignant was a session with my patient Robert, now in his mid-fifties, who looked in the mirror one day and hardly recognised himself (like Freud). The white roots of his hair, for years dyed, were showing and his shame about aging made him feel that he could not recognise himself. To this owner of a business dominated by twenty-somethings, a poet and master of Oedipal fantasy and metaphor, I made the following concrete remark: "Your hair grows in quickly, doesn't it?" This odd moment for Robert of bodily shame had its "roots" in having been mothered by a society lady who was always "out to lunch".

Most people experience some shame as the body changes and ages and then learn to adapt to it. Extreme cases of those who do not have been described by Phillips (1996) in her book *The Broken Mirror*. She coined the term "body dysmorphic disorder" (BDD) and chronicled the plight of patients she had treated who tortured themselves, like Sartre, in their relationship to mirrors, feeling stuck to them for hours, compelled to stand and look. One found it hard to function because of the need to comb and recomb her hair. It was difficult for her to perform her work in a hospital because the patients' rooms had mirrors. She tried to conquer this problem by getting dressed without her contact lenses so that she could not see and could avoid mirrors.

Third case vignette

Let me end with one last example: Robin, an elegant wealthy woman, was plagued by her body, which seemed to me anorectic, yet she worried if she gained a pound. She was 5'5" tall and weighed 105 pounds. She was constantly being shamed by others, who told her that she was too thin. Robin was obsessed with her clothes and spent close to $100,000 a year on her wardrobe. Yet she felt that she had nothing to wear and spent hours in front of her closets in each of her four homes not being able to decide what to wear or what to pack for the house she was travelling to next. Her greatest dread was of the shame she would feel if she went somewhere and confronted, all of a sudden, another woman who was better dressed, who "really" knew how to put her outfit together. If well-dressed women were wearing extremely pointy boots that day, she was compelled to go to a store and purchase similar boots. She was terrified of being the recipient of envy of the kind she herself experienced and often would not wear her best clothes for that reason.

Robin seemed to suffer from an internalisation of an envious critic appearing in the guise of a harsh superego introject. Incidentally, a series of women I have seen in psychotherapy with issues like Robin's have been endless talkers, are on their cell phones a good part of the day, and lead frenetically busy lives. Robin endured ongoing humiliation by her husband, who would not listen to her, she being a "motor mouth" who invited his constant rejection. Robin maintained an exhaustingly busy schedule filled with minutiae and chores. She defended against experiencing feelings of shame by "not thinking". At the beginning of treatment she brought in lists of things to tell me, clippings from self-help articles, sorting and shuffling among them in her Hermes handbag, so that I would notice the bag. Once she told me what was in the notes, she threw them away, nothing really being processed by her. She came in once asking to use the bathroom and quipped that it was one of many in the city she used all day. Robin's problems are rather typical of a certain type of woman who seeks analytic treatment but needs a treatment geared to her concreteness.

Rizzuto (1988) noted that patients such as Robin "deal with the spoken word as though it is an indispensable but meaningless nuisance that they have no choice but to use. Frequently the affective tone of their voice is a monotone pitch which may disclaim the significance of the content of what they are saying …. When the analyst speaks trying to help the patient to understand herself, he or she is frequently met with an attitude of disbelief, scepticism, and rejection of what the meaning might be" (p. 1).

Farrell (2000) decided on her book's title *Lost for Words*, recognising that words are problematic for women with eating disorders. "They are either seen as a useless form of communication, or as tremendously powerful, so powerful that they may drown in them, or be torn to pieces by them. The pre-verbal, concrete way these women often think and relate make words both a dangerous and unwanted commodity" (p. xiv). Farrell sees the body for such women as a transitional object. Their mothers have taken *them* as objects rather than the other way around. "She wishes to use her baby both to confirm her own physical boundaries and as a bridge toward whole object relations" (p. 44). This certainly seems to be the case with Amanda.

To conclude: the analysis of body narcissism is a painful and difficult task. It opens up all kinds of fantasies and memories related to shame and humiliation and sometimes mental, physical and sexual abuse. Too rapid a leap from the concrete can unleash a sadistic attack on the analyst, a therapeutic "bloodbath" from which it may be difficult to recover, or more likely, without the words being expressed, an abrupt termination. The analyst's countertransference must be constantly monitored. It is very hard work.

References

Brunswick, R. M. (1928). A supplement to Freud's history of an infantile neurosis. *International Journal of Psychoanalysis*, 9: 439–476.

Caper, R. (1994). What is a clinical fact? *International Journal of Psychoanalysis*, 75: 903–913.

Farrell, E. (2000). *Lost for Words: The Psychoanalysis of Anorexia and Bulimia*. New York: Other Press.

Freud, S. (1919h). *The Uncanny*. S. E., 17. London: Hogarth.

Freud, S. (1923b). *The Ego and the Ed*. S. E., 19. London: Hogarth.

Gilman, S. (1995). *Picturing Health and Illness: Images of Identity and Difference*. Baltimore, MD: Johns Hopkins Press.

Gilman, S. (1998). *Creating Beauty to Cure the Soul: Race and Psychology in the Shaping of Cosmetic Surgery*. Durham, NC: Duke University Press.

Jacobs, T. (2005). Presentation at the Psychoanalytic Association of New York.

Jay, M. (1993). *Downcast Eyes: The Denigration of Vision in Twentieth Century French Thought*. Berkeley, CA: University of California Press.

Lieberman, J. S. (2000). *Body Talk: Looking and Being Looked at in Psychotherapy*. Northvale, NJ: Jason Aronson.

Lieberman, J. S. (2006). Presentation in panel on "Shame and the Body". Symposium 2006: Shame, Mount Sinai Hospital, New York.

Lombardi, R. (2003). Catalyzing the dialogue between the body and the mind in a psychotic analysand. *Psychoanalytic Quarterly*, 72: 1017–1041.

Lombardi, R. (2008). The body in the analytic session: focusing on the body-mind link. *International Journal of Psychoanalysis*, 89: 89–110.

Mitrani, J. (2007). Bodily centered protections in adolescence: an extension of the work of Frances Tustin. *International Journal of Psychoanalysis*, 88: 1153–1169.

Phillips, K. A. (1996). *The Broken Mirror*. New York: Oxford University Press.

Rizzuto, A.-M. (1988). Transference, language and affect in the treatment of bulimarexia. *International Journal of Psychoanalysis*, 69: 369–387.

Steiner, J. (2006). Seeing and being seen: narcissistic pride and narcissistic humiliation. *International Journal of Psychoanalysis*, 87: 939–951.

INDEX

narcissistic parenting 104
naysayer 78
negative capability 88
neurotic anxiety 26
non-pathological concrete thinking
    clinical examples 95–98
    ordinary (non-clinical) example
        93–95
normative concretising function 4

object constancy 120
object relations theory 74
Ogden, T. 12, 37, 43
organisations 73–75, 80 *see also*:
    bureaucratisation of thought/
    language

pairing (baP) 77
paranoid-schizoid position 80
    and depressive positions
        86–89
    concrete thinking in 90–93
Parnes, D. 95
Phillips, K. 121, 130
Piaget, J. 73, 85
Poitier, S. 93–94
Pontalis, J. B. xx
possibility of meaning 17, 19
pre-Oedipal world xxiv
projective identification 5, 87
Proust, M. xxvii
pseudo-concreteness 84
psychic development 89
psychic reality 43–44, 59
psychoanalyst 85, 121
psychoanalytic process xxi, 35
psychoanalytic theorizing 122
psychodynamics xxiii
psychologists, developmental 85

Racker, H. 50
reality of castration 19

reflective thought 2–3, 15 *see also*:
    concretisation
Reich, A. 63
Renik, O. 57, 84
repression xxv
re-traumatisation 14
Rizzuto, A. -M. 122, 132
Rothstein, A. xxiv
Russell, J. 41

Sandell xxviii
Sandler, J. 47
Sandler, P. C. 4–5
Sanville, J. 36
Sartre, Jean-Paul 120
Schimek xxii
schizoid states of mind 80
schizophrenic man 85
Searles, H. xix, xxi, 73, 84–85, 90, 92
Segal, H. 58, 85, 87, 91–92
self, distress-based 2
self-neglect 10
self-object differentiation 92
self-preservative function 18
sense of aliveness 64
sense-perceptions 92
sensory experience 2–3
separateness 63
sexual dysfunction 120
shame 28
    experience 121
    language-deficient 121
Silverman, D. 41
social psychology 74
speaking 59
Steiner, J. 18, 36, 122
Steingart, I. xxiv, 36, 42
Stern, D. B. 48, 58, 69
structuralisation 36, 51
subjectivity 43
superego 6, 25
symbol formation 79, 86

For Product Safety Concerns and Information please contact our EU
representative GPSR@taylorandfrancis.com
Taylor & Francis Verlag GmbH, Kaufingerstraße 24, 80331 München, Germany

www.ingramcontent.com/pod-product-compliance
Lightning Source LLC
Chambersburg PA
CBHW050609280326
41932CB00016B/2966